AF333541

Recommended
COUNTRY HOTELS
OF BRITAIN
1989

INCLUDING COUNTRY
HOUSE HOLIDAYS

Accommodation, cuisine, service
and amenities
in Country Hotels and Country Houses
of distinction

Editorial Consultant
PETER STANLEY WILLIAMS

FHG PUBLICATIONS
A Herald Holiday Handbook

Planning a Break . . . ?

Enjoy a relaxing **5 Day Cornish Heritage** or **Cornish Castles Holiday** with a choice of no less than **twelve** leading AA★★★RAC or superior AA★★RAC hotels ranging from 17th century waterside inns to character country houses. En-suite accommodation with a full Westcountry breakfast and dinner each day plus a year's **free** membership of either the **National Trust** or **English Heritage**.

Come to CORNWALL

Write or telephone
for a brochure NOW!

Virginia Perkins (RH),
Hospitality Hotels of Cornwall,
Presingoll House,
St. Agnes,
Cornwall TR5 0PA
Tel: St. Agnes (087255) 3655

For the best in Leisure Holidays

Herald Holiday Handbooks 1989
Recommended Country Hotels of Britain
Recommended Wayside Inns of Britain
Recommended Short-Break Holidays in Britain
Pets Welcome!
Bed and Breakfast in Britain

1989 Edition
ISBN 1 85055 092 1
© FHG Publications Ltd.
No part of this publication may be reproduced by any means or
transmitted without the permission of the Publishers.

Cartography by GEO projects (U.K.) Ltd., Henley-on-Thames
Maps are based on Ordnance Survey maps with the permission of
the Controller of Her Majesty's Stationery Office. Crown copyright reserved.

Typeset by R D Composition Ltd., Glasgow.
Printed and bound in Great Britain by Richard Clays, Bungay, Suffolk.
Distributed by John Bartholomew & Son Ltd., Duncan Street, Edinburgh EH9 1TA (031-667 9341).

Published by FHG Publications Ltd. (Benn Brothers),
Abbey Mill Business Centre, Seedhill, Paisley PA1 1JN (041-887 0428/9).
A member of the U.N. Group.

Cover design: Russell Design Associates
Cover picture: Pennyhill Park Hotel & Country Club.

———

US ISBN 1-55650-049-1
Distributed in the United States by
Hunter Publishing Inc., 300 Raritan Center Parkway, CN94,
Edison, N.J., 08818, USA

CONTENTS

Country Hotels

ENGLAND

WALES

SCOTLAND

Recommended
COUNTRY HOTELS
OF BRITAIN
1989

With encouraging signs of economic recovery and cautious indications that holidays in Britain might expect some growth, the well-run country house hotel need have no fears for the future. Far-sighted proprietors and managers have invested in quality, they have built on traditions of hospitality and service and have already found an appreciative market.

The 1989 edition of RECOMMENDED COUNTRY HOTELS OF BRITAIN continues to display the tremendous variety of style and character amongst what might be regarded as a very traditional type of accommodation. We are happy to include once again distinctive favourites like the very old and beautifully timbered *Dog and Partridge Hotel* at Tutbury, Staffordshire; the impressive Victorian mansion of *Letham Grange* near Arbroath in Scotland with its golf course and curling rink; the large and luxurious *Selsdon Park Hotel* only 30 minutes from Central London and the much smaller but equally well-endowed *Mill House Hotel* in West Sussex.

To add to your choice this year we welcome such widespread new entries as the *Hospitality Inns* of Cornwall, *Little Orchard House* in Rye, Sussex, *Bryn Cregin Garden Hotel* at Deganwy, Gwynedd, the *Langdale Hotel* in Cumbria, *Murrayshall Country House Hotel* near Perth and the *Grand Island Hotel* at Ramsey on the Isle of Man.

Because we go to press early and there are often a range of booking and price options, rates for individual hotels are rarely quoted. It would be wrong to conclude that costs are at all prohibitive and we know that even in high season, excellent value for money is available. Please check terms and other details before booking. Although we cannot accept responsibility for the accommodation or services described in the pages that follow, please let us know if you have a disappointing experience or any serious problem which has not been settled on the spot. We will follow it up.

Our rich resource in fine country house hotels is appreciated abroad as well as in Britain. The growing readership for RECOMMENDED COUNTRY HOTELS in the United States is an impressive example. What excellent taste this shows!

We are delighted to help promote the benefits of all the establishments which fill the pages that follow. Such good news deserves to be spread as widely as possible.

Peter Clark
Publishing Director

Avon

THE OLD MILL HOTEL AND RESTAURANT,
Tollbridge Road, Bath,
Avon BA1 7DE

Tel: 0225 858476

Licensed; 15 bedrooms, all with private bathrooms; Historic interest; Children welcome; Car park (35); Bristol 13 miles.

What could be more luxurious than enjoying yourself in the relaxed and picturesque setting of the Old Mill Hotel, set on the banks of the River Avon, bridge and with fishing facilities. The hotel offers luxurious accommodation of en suite bedrooms, most with breathtaking river views. All rooms have colour television, telephone and some with four-poster beds. Also available is the Riverside à la Carte Restaurant and fully licensed bar. Interesting and varied bar meals and business lunches. Situated only 5 miles from city centre. *ETB* 🌸 🌸 🌸, *RAC***.

Please mention
Recommended COUNTRY HOTELS
when seeking refreshment or
accommodation at a Hotel
mentioned in these pages

COMBE GROVE MANOR,
Brassknocker Hill, Bath,
Avon BA2 7HS

Tel: 0225 834644

Licensed; 44 bedrooms, all with private bathrooms; Historic interest; Children welcome; Car park (200); Bristol 13 miles.

With a readily acquired reputation for its magnificent leisure facilities, this gracious eighteenth century house is surrounded by 68 acres of formal gardens and woodland in which, discreetly placed, are opportunities to delight the most ardent sports fanatic, which operate under the banner of the Cannons Country Club. These fine amenities offer an almost bewildering choice of activities and include golf, pitch and putt and driving range, tennis courts, bowls, indoor and outdoor swimming pools, squash courts, jogging track, sauna, solarium and much more. Overlooking the lovely Limpley Stoke Valley and only a short walk from the beauties of Bath, the hotel satisfies exercise-sharpened appetites in its superb à la carte restaurant under the expert supervision of a skilled chef. There is also a private dining room and a welcoming wine bar and restaurant with a terraced garden. Delightfully decorated public rooms include a comfortable drawing room and a grand staircase leads to the guest rooms, each of which is individually furnished to a high standard of style and practicality. Among the many luxuries to enjoy are bathrooms with jacuzzis. Suites are also available with separate sitting rooms. With a range of sporting amenities, unparalleled in our experience, allied to superlative comforts, this is a holiday retreat truly 'par excellence'.

HOMEWOOD PARK HOTEL,
Hinton Charterhouse, Bath,
Avon BA3 6BB

Tel: 022-122 3731*

Restaurant licence; 15 bedrooms, all with private bathrooms; Children welcome; Car park (30); Bristol 11 miles.

Informal luxury is the theme of this large and charming country house set in lovely countryside, only five miles from Bath. Constructed in the eighteenth century and considerably enlarged in Victorian times, Homewood Park is now a superbly decorated country hotel of distinction, thanks to the ministrations of Proprietors Stephen and Penny Ross. Not only are the guest rooms worthy of special comment but the cuisine has been widely recommended for its excellence and originality. The house is situated in 10 acres of woodland and gardens where there is a tennis court and croquet lawn. Facilities for golf and riding exist nearby. There are well-equipped meeting rooms for private functions.

NOTE

All the information in this book is given in good faith in the belief that it is correct. However, the publishers cannot guarantee the facts given in these pages, neither are they responsible for changes in policy, ownership or terms that may take place after the date of going to press. Readers should always satisfy themselves that the facilities they require are available and that the terms, if quoted, still apply.

BATCH FARM COUNTRY HOTEL,
Lympsham, Near Weston-super-Mare, Avon

Tel: 093-472 371*

Restaurant and residential licence; 8 bedrooms, all with private bathrooms; Historic interest; Children welcome; Car park (50); Burnham-on-Sea 4 miles.

An air of old world charm pervades Batch Farm lending atmosphere to the modern accommodation. Guests are welcome here all year except Christmas, and the eight bedrooms (all en suite) are comfortably fitted and have colour TV and teasmade. All enjoy panoramic views of hills and countryside. For guests' relaxation there is a fully licensed lounge bar, games room, and three lounges, one with colour TV. Traditional home cooking using local produce and home reared beef when possible is offered in the à la carte restaurant. Fishing is available in the grounds, and riding, swimming, tennis, and golf are to be found locally. Batch Farm is ideal for touring, being three miles from sea and sands and midway between Weston and Burnham-on-Sea, with Cheddar, Wells, Longleat, Bristol and Bath all in easy reach. Personal attention from the resident proprietors will ensure that your holiday is a happy one. Brochure. *AA**, RAC**; Egon Ronay, Ashley Courtenay Recommended.*

RANGEWORTHY COURT HOTEL,
Church Lane, Rangeworthy, Bristol, Avon BS17 5ND

Tel: 045-422 347*

Residential and restaurant licence; 14 bedrooms, 11 with private shower-rooms; Historic interest; Children welcome; Car park (50); Bath 20 miles, Bristol 12.

A family owned country house hotel dating from the fourteenth century in which the happy ambience of days gone by is still retained. Comforts in line with modern requirements have been skilfully introduced in keeping with good service and first-class food. Bedrooms are well equipped, each having television, direct-dial telephone and tea and coffee-makers and there are two lounges, one adjacent to the bar and the other for residents only. Set in peaceful and beautiful gardens, the old house is conveniently near the Severn Bridge and the M4 and M5 motorways. There are facilities for wedding receptions and small day conferences. *AA, RAC**. ETB* 🌹 🌹 🌹.

---

* The appearance of an asterisk after the telephone number indicates that the hotel in question is closed for a period during the winter months. Exact dates should be ascertained from the hotel itself.

STON EASTON PARK,
Ston Easton, Near Bath,
Avon BA3 4DF

Tel: 076-121 631 Telex: 444738 (Avostl G)

Restaurant and residential licence; 20 bedrooms, all with private bathrooms; Historic interest; Children over 12 years welcome; Car park (60), garage (2); Bristol 14 miles, Wells 8.

Ston Easton Park is a Listed Grade I Palladian mansion containing some of the most exceptional architectural and decorative features of its period to be found in the West Country. It has undergone extensive restoration capturing the elegance and splendour of the eighteenth century, and the bedrooms have been comfortably furnished, each with its own private bathroom, and colour television, radio and telephone. Several rooms have four poster beds which overlook the romantic parklands created in 1793 by Humphrey Repton. The main diningroom, formerly the old parlour, has become a friendly yet elegant restaurant. The consistently high standard of the menu blends a subtle choice of English and French dishes. The house cellars have been restocked to include a fine selection of rare wines and old vintages. Ston Easton Park received the Egon Ronay Gold Plate Award for the Hotel of the Year 1982.

THORNBURY CASTLE,
Thornbury,
Avon BS12 1HH

Tel: 0454 418511* Telex: 449986

Restaurant licence; 18 bedrooms, all with private bathrooms; Historic interest; Children over 12 years welcome; Car park (50); Bristol 15 miles; junction of M4/M5 motorway 5 miles.

Once owned by Henry VIII, this beautiful Tudor Castle offers a truly unique holiday opportunity to its guests. There are 18 luxury bedchambers, some with four poster beds and oriel windows overlooking the gardens and vineyard. Most sports are available nearby, while croquet may be played on the hotel lawn. Ideally placed for visits to the Georgian city of Bath, the Cotswolds, the Wye Valley and Stratford-upon-Avon. Personally guided tours available. Recipient of RAC's prestigious 'Blue Ribbon' Award. Highly rated by AA (3 red stars and rosette), Michelin and Good Food Guide. Winterbreak package available — details on request.

Berkshire

MANOR HOTEL,
The Village Green, Datchet, Near Windsor, Berkshire SL3 9EA

Tel: 0753 43442

Licensed; 30 bedrooms, all with private bathrooms; Children and dogs welcome; Car park (30); London 23 miles, Slough 3.

We found this attractive hotel five minutes upstream from Windsor and were immediately impressed by its position overlooking the village green and its convenience for so many places of sporting and historic interest. The handsome lounge bar is obviously popular with residents and locals alike and a visit to the intimate cocktail bar is recommended before settling down with other contented diners in a restaurant which boasts a marvellously varied à la carte menu. Well up to the high standards set by the Calotels group, guest rooms are superbly appointed and the Royal Suite offers first-class function facilities. The hotel is within easy reach of Heathrow Airport and London's West End and the multifarious pleasures of the Thames are virtually on the doorstep.

THE COPPER INN,
Pangbourne-on-Thames, Reading, Berkshire RG8 7AR

Tel: 073-57 2244

Licensed; 21 bedrooms, all with private bathrooms; Children welcome; Car park (25); Oxford 22 miles, Reading 6.

Built as a coaching inn called 'The Elephant' in the nineteenth century, this lovely retreat on the River Thames has grown and prospered to become the elegant hotel it is today, serving tourists and businessmen with equal merit, such is its ease of access from London. Amenities old and new combine in sweet harmony and all the guest rooms now have private bathrooms, colour television, radio and direct-dial telephone. In recent years, a considerable reputation has been built up for the excellence of the cuisine, fresh produce of the highest standard exhibiting flair and expertise and backed by smiling service. Lunchtime refreshment is available in an attractive bar serving imaginative snacks and real ale.

ROMANS HOTEL,
Little London Road, Silchester,
Berkshire RG7 2PN
Tel: 0734 700421*

Licensed; 24 bedrooms, all with private bathrooms; Children and dogs welcome; Car park (40); Reading 11 miles, Basingstoke 9.

Silchester was an important place in Roman times and this appropriately named hotel is just as important to discerning travellers of the modern age. Delightfully furnished throughout, the house was stylishly built at the turn of the century and the charm of the period is plainly evident as it exists happily alongside wonderful contemporary amenities. All bedrooms have en suite facilities, teletext television, direct dial telephone, radio alarm, tea and coffee makers and trouser press. The varied restaurant menu is changed daily and we can confirm it is well patronised. There is also a spruce, self-contained conference suite and rooms for smaller functions. In the mature and colourful gardens are two hard court tennis courts and a heated outdoor swimming pool.

TAPLOW HOUSE HOTEL,
Taplow, Maidenhead,
Berkshire SL6 0DA
Tel: 0628 70056
Fax: (0628) 773625 Telex: 848522 TAPLOW G

Licensed; 28 bedrooms, all with private bathrooms; Historic interest; Children and dogs welcome; Car park (80); Slough 4 miles.

One of the most popular and pleasantly placed venues in the Thames Valley, this appealing country house is beautifully appointed and offers the ultimate in comfort and amenities. With an enviable reputation for its first-rate cuisine, the hotel is also in great demand for conferences and private functions for which it is splendidly equipped. The grounds, in which there are many rare trees, contribute to a relaxed frame of mind and the guest rooms are spacious and elegantly decorated, each being equipped with en suite facilities, colour television, radio, direct-dial telephone and tea and coffee-makers. Special terms for weekend bookings.

> * The appearance of an asterisk after the telephone number indicates that the hotel in question is closed for a period during the winter months. Exact dates should be ascertained from the hotel itself.

Cheshire

THE OLD HALL,
Madeley, Near Crewe,
Cheshire

Tel: 0782 750209

5 bedrooms, 3 with private bathrooms; Historic interest; Children welcome; Car park; Stoke-on-Trent 6 miles.

Attractive 400 year old timbered building of great character and historic interest locally, with carved inscription. Situated in large attractive gardens with tennis court, ornamental pool and croquet lawn for visitors' enjoyment. It provides very comfortable accommodation — 3 bedrooms en suite, family and double room. Tea/coffee making facilities, television, central heating. Delicious vegetarian, wholefood and traditional meals by arrangement. Situated close to Potteries and the two largest garden centres in Europe. *ETB* 🌸 🌸.

ALVASTON HALL HOTEL,
Middlewich Road, Nantwich,
Cheshire CW5 6PD

Tel: 0270 624341

Licensed; 90 bedrooms, all with private bathrooms; Historic interest; Children welcome, dogs by arrangement; Car park (300); London 171 miles, Chester 20, Stoke-on-Trent 14, Crewe 4.

Set in 15 acres of rolling Cheshire countryside the Alvaston Hall Hotel is one of the finest hotel venues in south Cheshire. Close to the beautiful medieval town of Nantwich it is easily accessible by road and rail. The hotel offers a plethora of activities, including swimming, whirlpool bath, tennis, squash, steam rooms, sauna, solarium, and multi gym—all are available in the Leisure Complex. Guests can also take advantage of tennis courts situated within the grounds. Restaurants offer only the finest fresh food available and a choice of bars ensures complete relaxation and enjoyment. Special weekend breaks available.

ROOKERY HALL,
Worleston, Near Nantwich,
Cheshire CW5 6DQ

Tel: 0270 626866*

Licensed; 11 bedrooms, all with private bathrooms; Historic interest; Children over 10 welcome; Car park (50); Crewe 4 miles, Nantwich 2.

Although Georgian in origin, this fine country house was subsequently transformed into a baronial chateau in the late nineteenth century. This Grade II Listed Building stands resplendent in 28 acres of glorious gardens and woods alongside which runs the River Weaver. The house has many rich features of architectural interest and today, with the nineteenth-century estate restored under Select Country Hotels' ownership, it has acquired the reputation of being one of the best regarded hotels in the country for cuisine and service. Strolling in the grounds is a rewarding pastime and one may play tennis and croquet.

Cleveland

CRATHORNE HALL HOTEL,
**Crathorne, Yarm,
Cleveland TS15 0AR**

Tel: 0642 700398

Licensed; 39 bedrooms, all with private bathrooms; Historic interest; Children and dogs welcome; Car park (100); Stockton-on-Tees 10 miles.

A trifle awe-inspiring to the eye, this immense Edwardian house hides amenities that belong to the highest echelons. Beautifully furnished in period style, public and private rooms look out over 15 acres of grounds to the Leven Valley and the Cleveland Hills beyond. The drawing rooms displays a magnificent coat-of-arms fireplace and fine carved woodwork which is also a feature of the distinctive cocktail bar. Spacious and tastefully appointed bedrooms satisfy every modern demand, each having private bathroom, colour television, radio and telephone, whilst the English and Continental cuisine, well supported by an extensive wine list, achieves a rare standard of eminence. The hotel has a games room and excellent facilities for conferences.

PLEASE ENCLOSE A STAMPED ADDRESSED ENVELOPE WHEN WRITING TO ENQUIRE ABOUT ACCOMMODATION FEATURED IN THIS GUIDE

Cornwall

WENN MANOR HOTEL,
St. Wenn, Near Bodmin,
Cornwall

Tel: 0726 890240*

Restaurant and residential licence; 9 bedrooms, 8 with private bathrooms; Children welcome; Car park; Truro 25 miles, Newquay 20.

Although within easy reach of major towns and both Cornish coasts, this attractive Georgian house beckons lovers of peace and quiet for its situation in 4 acres of wooded grounds is idyllic. Centrally heated throughout, the hotel is very well appointed with two lounges, one with colour television and the other with a bar, dart board and other games. A variety of appetising table d'hôte dishes is on offer in the large dining room which overlooks the croquet lawn, supplemented by a good selection of wines. In a secluded corner of the garden is a heated swimming pool and there is also a putting green.

WILLAPARK MANOR HOTEL,
Bossingey, Near Tintagel,
Cornwall PL34 0BA

Tel: 0840 770782

Restaurant and residential licence; 14 bedrooms, all with private bathrooms; Children and pets welcome; Camelford 4 miles.

Beautiful character house, perched on the cliffs amidst 14 acres landscaped gardens and secluded woodland overlooking the Bay. Direct access to coast path and beach with wonderful walks in every direction. 14 bedrooms, all en suite, with colour television and tea makers. Excellent cuisine, well stocked cocktail bar and a uniquely friendly and informal atmosphere. *ETB* ♛ ♛ ♛.

CRACKINGTON MANOR,
Crackington Haven,
Cornwall EX23 0JG

Tel: 084-03 397/536

Licensed; 15 bedrooms, 12 with private bathrooms; Children and dogs welcome; Car park (25);
Launceston 19 miles, Bude 10, Camelford 9.

This friendly country hotel set in three and a half acres of grounds, is beautifully situated between two National Trust headlands and is just a hundred yards from the sea. Bedrooms are individually styled, most having en suite facilities. Family rooms and family suites are also available. All food is freshly prepared and menus, changed daily, are complemented by a good wine list. Facilities include a heated outdoor pool, sauna, solarium, multi-gym facilities games room and child-listening service. Riding, golf, tennis, fishing and spectacular coastal walks are all close at hand. Visa and Access are accepted.

PENMERE MANOR HOTEL,
Mongleath Road, Falmouth,
Cornwall TR11 4PN

Tel: 0326 314545

Licensed; 32 bedrooms, all with private bathrooms; Historic interest; Children and dogs welcome; Car park (50); Truro 11 miles.

This fine Georgian Country House, situated in five acres of garden and woodland overlooking Falmouth Bay, is owned and managed by the Pope family. The elegant ambience of a country house is retained throughout and the lounges and Fountain Bar are peaceful and relaxing. Excellent food and wine in the restaurant accompanied by entertainment from our Grand Piano each evening. The attractive bedrooms are individually decorated and all have private facilities, colour television, hair dryer, clock radio, telephone and tea/coffee making equipment. The Fountain Leisure Club offers indoor and outdoor swimming pools, jacuzzi spa, solarium and many other leisure pursuits.

CRILL HOUSE HOTEL,
Lower Crill, Falmouth,
Cornwall TR11 5BL

Tel: 0326 312994

Restaurant and residential licence; 11 bedrooms, all with private bathrooms; Children and dogs welcome; Car park (22); Land's End 35 miles, Truro 10, Falmouth 2.

Tucked away down a winding country lane Crill House offers the peace and quiet of a sheltered valley just two miles from the centre of Falmouth. Set in its own grounds with beautiful gardens the hotel is within easy walking distance of coastal footpaths and the relaxing country walks for which Cornwall is so famous. All the luxurious bedrooms have bathrooms en suite together with colour television and tea and coffee making facilities. Personally run by the Fenton family, Crill House prides itself on its high standards of service and relaxing, informal atmosphere. The modestly priced wine list complements the five course evening meal to complete the day's enjoyment. All this has earned the hotel AA Merit Awards for hospitality and bedrooms. Heated outdoor swimming pool.

CORMORANT HOTEL,
Golant, Fowey,
Cornwall

Tel: 072-683 3426

Residential and restaurant licence; 11 bedrooms, all with private bathrooms; Children and dogs welcome; Car park; Fowey 2 miles.

Perched 70 feet above the tidal reaches of the Fowey River, the Cormorant Hotel provides beautiful views from all its rooms of this source of excellent salmon and sea bass fishing. It offers a high standard of accommodation, all bedrooms having en suite bathroom and colour TV, while the restaurant is renowned for its superb cuisine. One delightful feature of the hotel is the heated swimming pool which has sliding glass doors and a motorised roof to allow for all moods of the weather. Golant is an unspoilt village with local facilities for sailing, fishing, and golfing as well as country walks and sandy beaches. *ETB* ♛ ♛ ♛

TREDETHY COUNTRY HOTEL,
Helland Bridge, Bodmin,
Cornwall PL30 4QS

Tel: 020-884 262/364

Restaurant and residential licence; 11 bedrooms, all with private bathrooms; Historic interest; Children welcome; Car park (30); Launceston 22 miles, Bodmin 3.

All the many attractions of the Royal Duchy may be reached with comparative ease from this comfortable and tranquil holiday retreat. Superbly placed in a verdant valley on the western side of Bodmin Moor, the hotel and its self-catering cottages stand in 9 acres of grounds embellished with shrubs and trees and in which lies a sheltered swimming pool. With magnificent, far-reaching views, this is a lovely place in which to relax. Each guest room has en suite amenities, colour television and telephone and the lounge (heated by a log fire) and dining room are just as charming and warmly welcoming. Excellent facilities exist nearby for riding, sailing, river and sea fishing and golf.

NANSLOE MANOR HOTEL,
**Meneage Road, Helston,
Cornwall TR13 0SB**   Tel: 0326 574691*

Restaurant and residential licence; 7 bedrooms, all with private bathrooms; Historic interest; Children over 10 years and dogs welcome; Car park (40); Penzance 13 miles.

Approached by a long drive through the woods, gracious Nansloe Manor is one of the finest small country hotels in Cornwall; what is more its friendly ambience is promoted by Cornish owners, Angela and Harry Davy Thomas. Beautifully decorated with panache and an eye to harmonious colour schemes, this most comfortable house stands in 4½ acres of tree-embowered grounds, a really peaceful setting for a relaxing holiday to remember. The guest rooms are a delight and each has a private bathroom or shower, colour television, telephone, hair dryer and tea and coffee-making facilities. The charming à la carte restaurant, which overlooks the croquet lawn, has acquired something of a reputation for its excellence and there is a well-stocked bar and cellar.

LAMORNA COVE HOTEL,
**Lamorna, Near Penzance,
Cornwall TR19 6XH**   Tel: 0736 731411/731030

Restaurant and residential licence; 18 bedrooms, all with private bathrooms; Historic interest; Children and dogs welcome; Car park; Land's End 9 miles, Penzance 5 miles.

In a sheltered position overlooking one of Cornwall's most celebrated beauty spots, this charming luxury hotel is both elegant and attractive. Individually furnished guest rooms all have private bathrooms and each is equipped with colour television, radio and direct-dial telephone; some are available with balconies to take full advantage of the fabulous views. There are three comfortable lounges and a popular sun lounge which overlooks the sea. Also in demand for moments of conviviality is the cocktail bar with its granite walls and abundance of copper. The gardens are bright and colourful, a perfect setting for the heated swimming pool. Dining here is a memorable experience, the menu specialising in home cooking and fresh produce.

MEUDON HOTEL,
**Mawnan Smith, Falmouth,
Cornwall TR11 5HT**   Tel: 0326 250541*

Residential and restaurant licence; 30 bedrooms, all with private bathrooms; Historic interest; Children over 5 welcome, dogs by arrangement; Car park; Redruth 14 miles, Truro 12, Falmouth 4.

The most picturesque part of the Cornish coast between the Fal and Helford Rivers is the enviable setting of this luxury hotel where the cuisine is something of a legend with locally caught sea-food especially worthy of mention. The beautifully landscaped gardens of 8 acres lead down to the sea and here one may relax in utter peace with rare flowering shrubs and plants providing a blaze of colour. Appointments throughout the hotel are of the highest standard and among the services available is a 24-hour hand laundry and a hairdressing salon. Free golf concessions exist nearby as well as opportunities for boating, riding, bowls, tennis, watersports and fishing.

> * The appearance of an asterisk after the telephone number indicates that the hotel in question is closed for a period during the winter months. Exact dates should be ascertained from the hotel itself.

TREGURRIAN HOTEL,
Watergate Bay, Near Newquay,
Cornwall

Tel: 0637 860280*

Restaurant and residential licence; 27 bedrooms, 20 with private bathrooms; Children and dogs welcome; Car park (26); Bodmin 20 miles.

Standing 100 yards from Watergate Bay's glorious sandy beach and spectacular Atlantic coastline is this splendid hotel. All 27 rooms have radio and baby listening, tea makers, and most are en suite. The hotel has a heated pool with sun patio, games room and solarium. There is an excellent choice of food with a good wine list. Licensed bar. Tregurrian is family run, and children are welcome at reduced rates. Centrally placed for touring all parts of Cornwall. *AA**.*

GOONHOSKYN,
Summer Court, Near Newquay,
Cornwall TR8 4PP

Tel: 0872 510226*

3 bedrooms; Children over 6 years welcome; Car park (4); Penzance 33 miles, Bodmin 20, Truro 16.

Clean and comfortable farmhouse set in rose gardens and pleasant rural surroundings with family atmosphere. The house is one mile from A30 towards Newquay and five miles from Newquay. All three bedrooms have washbasins and colour television. Separate sittingroom and diningroom. Good traditional home cooking is served with many Cornish flavours. Regret no pets or children aged under six years. *ETB* ♛ ♛.

DOWER HOUSE HOTEL,
Padstow,
Cornwall PL28 8BA

Tel: 0841 532317

Restaurant and residential licence; 9 bedrooms, 6 with private bathrooms; Historic interest; Children welcome, dogs by arrangement; Car park; Plymouth 46 miles, Newquay 15.

The Dower House is a friendly country house-style hotel set in beautiful surroundings with views of the Estuary and Deer Park, yet it is close to sandy beaches and the harbour. The Hotel's terrace has a sunny aspect and is an ideal spot in which to relax. Most rooms are fully en suite and all have beverage facilities. There is a TV lounge and bar lounge. The four course dinners are carefully chosen and personally prepared to provide varied menus and special diets are catered for. Off season rates are available. ETB 👑 👑.

LONG CROSS HOTEL,
Trelights, Near Port Isaac,
Cornwall PL29 3TF

Tel: 0208 880-243*

Licensed; 12 bedrooms, all with private bathrooms; Historic interest; Children and dogs welcome; Car park; London 239 miles, Exeter 67, Wadebridge 7.

An elegant late Victorian house standing in three acres of its own grounds and enjoying sweeping views over Cornwall's picturesque countryside and most spectacular coastline. Resident proprietors Janet and Roger Warrillow have done their best to ensure that Long Cross maintains its Victorian charm, from the delightful gardens and grounds to the elegant yet comfortably furnished public rooms. Quality is the hallmark, too, in the restaurant, where the emphasis is on English cuisine prepared from fresh produce and complemented by a reasonably priced wine list. Write or telephone for colour brochure. *AA***.

GLENEGLOS,
Trewint Lane, Rock,
Cornwall

Tel: 020-886 2369

Licensed; 6 bedrooms, 5 with private bathrooms; Children welcome; Car park (30); Camelford 14 miles, Wadebridge 7.

The aims of Pauline and Mick Burton are a warm, friendly atmosphere combined with personal service. Their small country-style hotel has comfortably-furnished bedrooms, most with en suite facilities, and all have television, tea/coffee making equipment, intercom and baby listening device. Freshly prepared meals in the traditional diningroom are complemented by a wide range of wines. The "old worlde" bar is the perfect spot to enjoy an aperitif or a relaxing drink after your meal. There is also a dry lounge and television area. Children are welcome but sorry, no pets. Terms from £25.00 per day for Bed, Breakfast and Evening Meal.

TREGIFFIAN HOTEL,
Sennen, Penzance,
Cornwall

Tel: 0736 871408*

Residential and restaurant licence; 8 bedrooms, all with private bathrooms, also 4 self-contained cottages and 4 studio flats; Children welcome; Car park; Penzance 8 miles, Land's End 2.

With sandy Sennen Cove immediately below and with far-reaching views towards the Isles of Scilly, this one-time farmhouse has been skilfully converted into a small but first-class hotel. Run under the benevolent eyes of Resident Proprietors Mr and Mrs A. Loutit, this charming house presents delightfully furnished accommodation, an elegant and comfortable lounge and a most attractive bar. All bedrooms have private facilities, radio/intercom and baby listening service. Cuisine is of a very high standard, with both table d'hôte and à la carte menus offering an appetising choice of dishes. The hotel stands in nearly two acres of grounds with numerous beauty spots within easy reach. This is an excellent place for those requiring a combined sea and country holiday. Dogs are accepted in the three ground-floor bedrooms only.

ROSE-IN-VALE COUNTRY HOUSE HOTEL,
Mithian, St. Agnes,
Cornwall TR5 0QD

Tel: 087-255 2202*

Restaurant and residential licence; 15 bedrooms, all with private bathrooms; Historic interest; Children and dogs welcome; Car park (40); Plymouth 60 miles, Perranporth 4.

Set in 11 acres of woodland and garden, the prettily named Rose-in-Vale has the dual advantages of the peace and quiet of the countryside whilst being within easy reach of the coast and many of the more popular tourist resorts. There is an informal, easy-going atmosphere about this little Georgian house; in the attractive diningroom where well-cooked food is presented with care and attention; in the comfortable lounges and cheerful bar; and on the sunny and sheltered terraces that overlook the swimming pool. All of the charmingly appointed guest rooms have en suite facilities, tea/coffee maker, telephone, and colour television available. Some have their own balcony.

BOSCUNDLE MANOR,
St. Austell,
Cornwall PL25 3RL

Tel: 072-681 3557*

Restaurant and residential licence; 11 bedrooms, all with private bathrooms; Historic interest; Children and dogs welcome; Car park (15); Truro 14 miles, Bodmin 13.

Andrew and Mary Flint have made the transition from city workers to hotel proprietors with inordinate success, even distinction. They fell in love with this beautiful 18th century manor house when they first came here in 1978 and have been improving the amenities ever since with flair and a keen appreciation of modern-day requirements. Antiques and paintings set off the attractive rooms and all the bedrooms in the main building and cottage annexe have en suite facilities, remote-control television and direct-dial telephone, whilst some have jacuzzi baths.

PORTH AVALLEN HOTEL,
Carlyon Bay, St. Austell,
Cornwall PL25 3SG

Tel: 072-681 2802*

Residential licence; 24 bedrooms, all with private bathrooms; Children welcome; Car park (50); London 241 miles, Plymouth 39, Truro 14, Bodmin 12, Fowey 9, Mevagissey 6.

Perhaps the most popular feature of this fine hotel is its magnificent view over Carlyon Bay, one of the most attractive indentations in the Cornish 'Riviera' coastline. In fact, the hotel's position offers the very best of all worlds — seaside, countryside and town, for St. Austell town centre is but a short distance away. Accommodation at 'Porth Avallen' is bright and airy; all 24 bedrooms have either bath or shower, colour television, telephone and teasmade; the residents' lounge is elegantly furnished with a period atmosphere and the diningroom is spacious and comfortable. In the latter, food of a high standard is served, having been prepared in the hotel's immaculate kitchens.

BOSSINEY HOUSE HOTEL,
Tintagel,
Cornwall PL34 0AX

Tel: 0840 770240*

Residential and restaurant licence; 20 bedrooms, 17 with private bathrooms; Children and dogs welcome; Car park (30); Bodmin 20 miles, Bude 19, Camelford 6.

At one time, Bossiney had its own mayor and corporation and in the sixteenth century Sir Francis Drake was one of its two M.P.s. Today a cluster of houses nestle close to a sandy cove with interesting rock formations, ideal for bathing, surfing or just unwinding. With wonderful cliff walks on either side this is the glorious situation of the beautifully-furnished Bossiney House Hotel, standing in grounds of two and a half acres. Guests may relax in the gardens, the indoor heated swimming pool, sauna and solarium, take in the sweeping sea views or try their skills on the putting green. Inside, one is immediately impressed by the spacious cleanliness of public and private rooms and, in particular, by the imaginative and pleasing colour schemes. This is a really happy place in which to stay and the proprietors and staff work hard to achieve this end. Pleasant lounges, one with a bar, are convivial meeting places in which to enjoy refreshment and the bedrooms are well appointed and make the most of sea and country views. In the catering department, fine English cooking is a feature of the menus offering excellent choice and variety. Quaint Tintagel is near at hand and the surrounding King Arthur's Country provides an almost bewildering choice of beauty spots, historic locations and sporting activities.

TREVAUNANCE POINT HOTEL,
Trevaunance Cove, St. Agnes,
Cornwall TR5 0RZ

Tel: 087-255 3235

Residential and restaurant licence; 2 double bedrooms, 5 twin/family bedrooms, 1 single bedroom; Children and dogs welcome; Car park (20); London 260 miles, Newquay 12, Truro 8, Redruth 7.

Take a step back in time and visit the centuries-old 'Trevaunance Point Hotel' nestling in clifftop gardens above the 'lost harbour of St. Agnes', its windows gazing seaward across the wide expanse of Perran Bay. Built from granite, local stone and slate and giant beams wrestled by wreckers from ill-fated ships, the hotel in summer becomes a cool oasis and, in winter, a warm and welcoming haven against the bracing and spectacular storms which oft' rage along this rugged Atlantic Coastline. Not this hotel for those who seek the plastic standards of the twentieth century—but good food in abundance, professional but friendly and courteous service, crackling log fires and candlelit dinners, the constant vocal accompaniment of the ever-moving sea, a pace of life and many other things you thought had long since been lost. The hotel is open all year and can be highly recommended for spring and autumn holidays. Bargain weekend breaks are available and a colour brochure may be obtained on request from Proprietor Marc Watts.

Cumbria

FISHERBECK HOTEL,
Lake Road, Ambleside,
Cumbria LA22 0DH

Tel: 05394 33215*

Licensed; 20 bedrooms, 18 with private facilities; Children welcome; Car park (20); Windermere 4 miles.

Half way between Ambleside and the Lake, this warm and welcoming hotel could scarcely be better placed for getting to know the wonders of the Lake District. Lake Winderemere is only five minutes' walk away and the rolling fells provide a scenic backdrop. Under the personal care of Proprietors Brian and Kathleen Barton, the hotel has an interesting history for it has been both a tannery and a school in its time. Converted into an attractively furnished holiday retreat, Fisherbeck offers comfortable accommodation of high standard, superb food and fine wines, while the original tannery is now a bar. *ETB* 🌹🌹🌹, *RAC and AA**, Ashley Courtenay recommended.*

KIRKSTONE FOOT COUNTRY HOUSE HOTEL,
Kirkstone Pass Road, Ambleside,
Cumbria LA22 9EH

Tel: 05394 32232

Residential and restaurant licence; 14 bedrooms, all with private bathrooms; 13 self-catering apartments; Children welcome; Car park (25); Penrith 30 miles, Keswick 17, Kendal 13.

Originally a seventeenth century manor house, this attractively furnished hotel stands in delightful, secluded grounds at the foot of one of Lakeland's most famous passes, yet it is conveniently only a few minutes' walk from Ambleside village, the ideal centre from which to explore the English Lake District. In their hotel, Jane and Simon Bateman have achieved their aim in providing superb food and gracious living in a convivial atmosphere and they are already renowned for their traditional English home cooking and fine cellar. Dining at the Kirkstone Foot is an experience you will long remember. Additionally, for those who prefer a greater degree of independence on holiday, there are several luxurious, self-contained apartments within the grounds of the hotel, each of which is fully equipped, including colour television and full central heating. Guests are welcome to enjoy all the amenities of the hotel and pets are welcome in the apartments. *BTA commended; ETB* 🌹 🌹 🌹 🌹.

LANGDALE HOTEL,
Great Langdale, Near Ambleside, Cumbria LA22 9JB

Tel: 09667 302

Licensed; 52 bedrooms, all with private bathrooms; Historic interest; Children welcome; Car park (130); Keswick 17 miles.

Charming Lake District hotel in 35 acres of beautifully landscaped grounds surrounded by breathtaking scenery. All 52 bedrooms have private facilities, colour television, radio, telephone and tea/coffee making facilities. Single rooms available. Babysitting service available. The hotel offers 3 bars, 3 restaurants, 2 lounges, games room, indoor swimming pool, sauna, steam room, 2 spa baths, plunge pool, solarium, fitness room, squash and badminton. Parking available. No dogs please. *AA/RAC****; ETB* 👑 👑 👑 👑 👑.

RIVERSIDE HOTEL,
Near Rothay Bridge, Under Loughrigg, Ambleside, Cumbria LA22 9LJ

Tel: 05-394 32395

Restaurant and residential licence; 10 bedrooms, all with private bathrooms; Historic interest; Children welcome; Car park (14); Windermere 4 miles.

Riverside Hotel is delightfully situated only a few minutes' walk from the centre of Ambleside, on a quiet country lane which runs alongside the River Rothay. There are extensive grounds with mature trees and shrubs and there is direct access onto Loughrigg Fell, which provides some of the most delightful walks in the Lake District and offers spectacular views over Windermere, Rydal Water and Grasmere. The hotel has been tastefully modernised throughout and offers ten bedrooms, all with private facilities, colour television and tea making facilities. There are three separate lounges, one of which leads onto a Garden Patio overlooking the river. The elegant restaurant offers meals of a very high standard, combining flair and imagination with the best of traditional and some Continental dishes. *AA, RAC***.

RECOMMENDED SHORT-BREAK HOLIDAYS
IN BRITAIN

Introduced by John Carter, TV Holiday Expert and Journalist

Specifically designed to cater for the most rapidly growing sector of the holiday market in the UK. Illustrated details of hotels offering special 'Bargain Breaks' throughout the year.

Available from newsagents and bookshops or direct from the publishers: £2.95 plus 30p postage.

FHG PUBLICATIONS LTD
Abbey Mill Business Centre, Seedhill,
Paisley, Renfrewshire PA1 1JN

ROTHAY GARDEN HOTEL,
Grasmere, Ambleside,
Cumbria LA22 9RH
Tel: 096-65 334*

Restaurant and residential licence; 16 bedrooms, all with private bathrooms; Children and dogs welcome; Car park (30); London 280 miles, Keswick 13, Windermere 9, Ambleside 4.

Our warm welcoming country house hotel is set in two acres of riverside gardens and offers quiet, well-appointed rooms that really do have views, some with four poster beds, exquisite linen and whirlpool baths. A comfortable bar and lounge with log fires and our very elegant restaurant together with Jackie's award winning cooking make for your comfort and well being. Wordsworth said of Grasmere 'The loveliest spot that man hath ever known.' May we send you our brochure? We look forward to meeting you.

APPLEBY MANOR COUNTRY HOUSE HOTEL,
Appleby-in-Westmorland,
Cumbria CA16 6JD
Tel: 076-83 51571

Licensed; 18 bedrooms, all with private bathrooms; Historic interest; Children and dogs welcome; Car park (40), garages (3); Kendal 24 miles, Penrith 13, Brough 8.

The county town of what was formerly Westmorland, Appleby is a cheerful little place where you will feel immediately at home, a quality shared by its finest three-star country house hotel—the Appleby Manor. Interesting and varied local cuisine features largely on the menu, presented in an intimate restaurant which enjoys fine views over the old castle and towards the Lakeland Fells. The fine indoor leisure club complete with swimming pool, sauna, spa bath and solarium, together with the guest rooms and public rooms which are appointed to a high degree of comfort, ensure that your 'Getaway Break' is as relaxing and refreshing as you could wish. *AA***, RAC****

RAVENSTONE HOTEL,
Bassenthwaite, Near Keswick,
Cumbria CA12 4QG   Tel: 059-681 240

Full licence; 15 bedrooms; Children welcome; Car park; Carlisle 25 miles, Penrith 20, Windermere 13, Keswick 5.

This truly lovely house, which was built by the Earl of Carlisle for Lady Charlotte Howard, is warm, tranquil, well-appointed, friendly, and flowers delight the eye everywhere. An immediate sense of welcome is heightened by cheerful log fires which augment the central heating. Known for its excellent cuisine and fresh produce, the hotel stands in beautiful surroundings on the slopes of Skiddaw and looks out over the valley towards the fells beyond Bassenthwaite Lake. There are plenty of diversions within the hotel itself, including a billiard room with full-size snooker table and a games room with table tennis. There is a pleasant bar and the enjoyment of meals is complemented by an interesting wine list and, last but not least, personal attention and very reasonable prices. High standards of appointment and service will ensure every satisfaction at this fine country hotel. En suite facilities, colour television, and tea-making facilities in all rooms.

BURN HOW GARDEN HOUSE HOTEL, MOTEL AND RESTAURANT,
**Bowness-on-Windermere,
Cumbria LA23 3HH**   Tel: 096-62 6226*

Residential and restaurant licence; 26 bedrooms, all with private bathrooms; Historic interest; Children welcome; Car park (35); London 271 miles, Penrith 26, Kendal 8, Ambleside 5.

Burn How is a unique combination of Victorian houses, modern chalets, and restaurant, offering elegance, comfort, and superb service. It is blessed with a secluded and peaceful setting in beautiful gardens in the heart of Bowness only two minutes' walk from both Lake and shops. The range of accommodation — from family rooms and traditional bedrooms to four poster suites — is well appointed and superbly fitted, with facilities for children and the disabled. The elegant restaurant specialises in English and French cuisine using only fresh produce, and the varied and imaginative menus are served with the extra personal attention which makes all the difference. Children's Menu, and Room Service for any meal. *AA***.*

LINTHWAITE COUNTRY HOUSE HOTEL,
**Bowness-on-Windermere,
Cumbria LA23 3JA**   Tel: 096-62 3688/2321*

Residential and restaurant licence; 11 bedrooms, all with private bathrooms; Car park (20); Penrith 26 miles, Kendal 8.

The mountain and lake views from this loftily perched hotel are spectacular, whilst visual pleasures abound in its own 14 acres of gardens and woodland where deer may sometimes be seen grazing. The grounds incorporate a putting green and private tarn for fishing. Delightfully secluded yet within easy strolling distance of tourist-popular Bowness, Linthwaite is a haven of tranquillity, offering elegant furnishings, the ultimate in comfort, a varied and noteworthy table d'hôte menu and, above all, the warmest of welcomes. The convivial bar promotes friendly conversation and sound repose is assured in well appointed guest rooms, all with private bathroom, colour television, radio, telephone and facilities for making hot drinks.

---

* The appearance of an asterisk after the telephone number indicates that the hotel in question is closed for a period during the winter months. Exact dates should be ascertained from the hotel itself.

LINDETH HOWE HOTEL,
Storrs Park, Bowness-on-Windermere,
Cumbria LA23 3JF

Tel: 096-62 5759*

Licensed; 14 bedrooms, all with private bathrooms; Historic interest; Kendal 9 miles, Windermere 1.

"A little gem hidden away" as quoted by Ashley Courtenay. The hotel occupies an impressive position overlooking Lake Windermere and stands in six acres of its own lovely grounds. Built in 1879, it was once the home of Beatrix Potter who bought it for her mother and where she spent many holidays enjoying its unrivalled views and idyllic location. Many of the rooms take advantage of the splendid views across the lake and all have colour television, radio, telephone, tea and coffee-making facilities and central heating. The elegant diningroom is the perfect place to enjoy a candlelit dinner with a tempting choice of exciting dishes, relaxing afterwards in the lounge over coffee by the log fire in the inglenook fireplace. And for the more energetic, the hotel has an exercise area, sauna and solarium. Short breaks available. *ETB* ♛ ♛ ♛ ♛, *Ashley Courtenay and Les Routiers recommended.*

LINDETH FELL COUNTRY HOUSE HOTEL,
Bowness-on-Windermere,
Cumbria LA23 3JP

Tel: 096-62 3286/4287*

Residential and restaurant licence; 15 bedrooms, all with private bathrooms; Children over 7 welcome; Car park; Lancaster 26 miles, Kendal 7.

Adhering firmly to a style and hospitality associated with a less hurried age, this fine hotel captures the elegance of days now sadly departed. In mellow surroundings, guests may relax in well-furnished rooms resplendent with oak-panelling and enjoy first-rate cuisine in the Cordon Bleu mode under the direct supervision of the gifted Diana Kennedy. The dining room has been extended to allow guests to take in views of the lake whilst dining and the landscaped gardens that surround the house add much to its atmosphere: here one may play tennis and croquet and there is also a putting green and a tarn on which guests may fish in hope and tranquillity. For a Lake District holiday, this hotel has much to commend it.

BORDRIGGS COUNTRY HOUSE HOTEL,
Longtail Hill, Bowness-on-Windermere,
Cumbria LA23 3LD

Tel: 096-62 3567*

Residential licence; 11 bedrooms, all with private bathrooms; Children over 10 welcome; Car park; Penrith 26 miles, Kendal 8.

Snugly set in beautiful gardens of 1½ acres amdist unspoilt, rolling countryside and with Windermere's 18-hole golf course just along the road, this gracious, well-appointed and family-run hotel is a fine headquarters for a rewarding and carefree Lakeland holiday with the promise of excellent food and wines for which the chef has acquired an enviable reputation. From all aspects, the public and private rooms are delightfully furnished, warm and welcoming. Bedrooms all have a private bathroom, colour television, clock/radio, hair dryer and direct-dial telephone and there are two en suite rooms on the ground floor for those who find the stairs difficult. Also on the ground floor is a family room with a double bed and two singles. With a terrace leading to a heated swimming pool, putting green and croquet lawn, the gardens offer opportunities for unexacting exercise. There are some 50 major events arranged to take place in the immediate area and many places of geographical and historical interest to visit. Only a gentle stroll away is Bowness Bay where boating, water-skiing, swimming, fishing and pleasure cruises may be enjoyed. Large enough to provide a high standard of amenities and service, Bordriggs is yet homely enough to ensure personal attention in a friendly and informal atmosphere.

MIDDLE RUDDINGS HOTEL,
Braithwaite, Keswick,
Cumbria CA12 5RY

Tel: 059-682 436*

Licensed; 14 bedrooms, 11 with private bathrooms; Car park (20), garage (2); Keswick 3 miles.

The Middle Ruddings Hotel is ideally located for touring and walking, set in over 2 acres of naturally landscaped Gardens nestling in the majestic scenery of the northern Lakes. Whichever part of this lovely House you settle in you'll feel cosseted in luxury and comfort. From your double or twin bedded en-suite room with television, radio and telephone and complimentary tea and coffee tray to the inviting tranquillity of the Lounge where you can relax far from the madding crowd, play Chess with fellow Guests or simply read from our extensive library. With that refeshing drink relax in the Lounge Bar enjoying the company of other like-minded Guests or retreat to the Garden Room — where the sun always shines — and indulge yourself in a Cream Tea with freshly baked Scones and Jam. Later, experience the pleasures of traditional French Cuisine served at its very best accompanied by fine wines in the candlelit Blossoms Restaurant. *ETB* 🌸 🌸 🌸 🌸.

HUNDITH HILL HOTEL,
Lorton Vale, Cockermouth,
Cumbria CA13 9TH

Tel: 0900 822092

Licensed; 20 bedrooms, 8 with private bathrooms; Historic interest; Children welcome, dogs by arrangement; Car park; London 318 miles, Carlisle 26, Keswick 13.

Superbly situated in the heart of Wordsworth country is this splendid Victorian house hotel run by resident proprietors Mr and Mrs Wallace, and offering a quiet and relaxing Lakeland centre for guests. Hundith Hill is close to Cockermouth and enjoys fine views of the beautiful Lorton Valley and Fells. Bedrooms are attractive and comfortable, and public rooms spacious and relaxing. The hotel has a small bar and a games room with darts, snooker and table tennis, while nearby outdoor pursuits include walking and climbing, fishing, sailing, pony trekking, and golf.

Available from most bookshops, the 1989 edition of THE GOLF GUIDE covers details of every UK golf course – well over 2000 entries – for holiday or business golf. Hundreds of hotel entries offer convenient accommodation, accompanying details of the courses – the 'pro', par score, length etc.

Sandy Lyle features on the front cover with golfing editorial from the Professional Golfers Association who also endorse the guide.

£4.95 from bookshops or £5.50 including postage from FHG Publications, Abbey Mill Business Centre, Paisley PA1 1JN.

ELTERMERE COUNTRY HOUSE HOTEL,
Elterwater, Near Ambleside,
Cumbria LA22 9HY
Tel: 096-67 207*

Residential and restaurant licence; 15 bedrooms, 12 with private bathrooms or showers; Historic interest; Children over 10 welcome, dogs by arrangement; Car park (20); London 279 miles, Windermere 8, Coniston 5, Ambleside 4

The still-unspoilt village of Elterwater is set in the Langdale Valley only a few miles from the head of Lake Windermere and the eighteenth century Eltermere Country House Hotel is well placed to take full advantage of its location right on the edge of the village overlooking the secluded tarn of Elterwater. Those who enjoy a personal welcome and attention, home cooked food and country-style comforts all laid on in a building of character and charm will certainly want to return again and again. The Eltermere has a well-equipped residents' bar and elegant diningroom where guests may enjoy sustenance in the evening. All the attractively furnished bedrooms have colour television and tea and coffee making facilities, and the hotel is centrally heated throughout. *AA, RAC**; Ashley Courtenay recommended; ETB* 🌸 🌸 🌸.

NETHERWOOD HOTEL,
Grange-over-Sands,
Cumbria LA11 6ET
Tel: 053-95 32552

Licensed; 23 bedrooms, 17 with private bathrooms; Historic interest; Children and dogs welcome; Car park (60); London 266 miles, Ulverston 15, Windermere 15, Kendal 14.

Gazing down over wooded slopes to the Morecambe Bay estuary, this country hotel by the sea reflects the high standards of comfort and opulence associated with its late nineteenth century origins. Not only did those responsible for the building have an eye for a choice site but the features and aspects of the builders' craftsmanship are lovingly retained in the house to this day, particularly in the carved oak fireplaces, panelling and fine high ceilings. The demands of a modern age have been introduced without spoiling the relaxing atmosphere to which log fires contribute from time to time. The varied cuisine exhibits expertise and skilful planning.

OVERWATER HALL,
Ireby, Near Bassenthwaite,
Cumbria CA5 1HH
Tel: 059-681 566*

Residential and restaurant licence; 13 bedrooms, all with private bathrooms; Historic interest; Children and dogs welcome; Car park; Newcastle-upon-Tyne 71 miles, Carlisle 17, Wigton 6.

Just two miles from Bassenthwaite Lake and in the shadow of Skiddaw (3100 ft.), this delightful building of architectural and historical interest has great character and lies peacefully in its 18 acres of secluded woodlands and gardens. This is a fine centre from which to explore the beauties of the Lake District and accommodation is well above average. The comfortable dining room presents a varied menu and guest rooms have en suite facilities as well as colour television, radio and excellent views. Relaxation may be sought in a spacious drawing room, cocktail bar, billiards room or on the sun terrace.

OLD CHURCH HOTEL,
Watermillock, Penrith,
Cumbria CA11 0JN
Tel: 085-36 204*

Restaurant and residential licence; 10 bedrooms, all with private bathrooms; Historic interest; Children welcome; Car park; Keswick 18 miles.

With extensive lawns running down to the shores of lovely Ullswater, this delightful country house is a peaceful headquarters from which to enjoy a relaxing Lakeland holiday. Built in 1754 on the site of a 12th century church, the house now performs a worthy function as a splendidly appointed hotel where guests will find comfort, good food, tranquillity and informality amidst glorious surroundings. Owners, Kevin and Maureen Whitemore, are to be congratulated on the decor and furnishings and the high standard of amenities.

RAMPSBECK HOTEL,
Watermillock, Ullswater,
Cumbria CA11 0LP
Tel: 085-36 442*

Licensed; 18 bedrooms, all with private bathrooms; Historic interest; Children and dogs welcome; Car park (30); Penrith 8 miles.

Charming early eighteenth century country house Hotel in 17 acres of ground situated on the shore of Lake Ullswater. Listed in the Egon Ronay Guide as one of the most beautifully situated hotels in Great Britain. Most bedrooms have lake views, all have private bathrooms, full central heating and are individually decorated and furnished. The restaurant, which overlooks the Lake, is open to non-residents and specialises in classical English cuisine with an emphasis on presentation. The hotel is within easy reach of many places of historic and local interest and facilities for pony trekking, fishing, sailing, wind surfing, golfing and climbing. It has achieved an AA Restaurant Rosette and is Egon Ronay and Ashley Courtenay Recommended.

WASDALE HEAD INN,
Wasdale Head,
Cumbria CA20 1EX
Tel: 094-06 229*

Licensed; 10 bedrooms, all with private bathrooms; Historic interest; Children and dogs welcome; Car park (50); London 305 miles, Whitehaven 21.

Standing in a unique and secluded setting at the head of Wasdale is this fine inn which embodies something of the spirit of adventure that attracted smugglers, mountaineers, and finally tourists to this valley, one of Lakeland's most remote and unspoilt. All the individually decorated bedrooms enjoy magnificent mountain views, while public rooms exude a warmth rarely found in the more stereotyped, chain hotels of today. The culinary emphasis is on good home cooking, with a hearty breakfast in the morning and five course table d'hôte in the evening. There is a wealth of leisure pursuits in this lovely area. *AA**, RAC**; ETB* 🌷 🌷 🌷.

COTTAGE IN THE WOOD,
Whinlatter Pass, Keswick,
Cumbria CA12 5TW

Tel: 059-682 409

Residential and restaurant licence; 9 bedrooms, 7 with private bathrooms; Historic interest; Car park (20); Cockermouth 8 miles, Buttermere 8, Keswick 4.

A charming eighteenth century former coaching inn beautifully and remotely situated atop Whinlatter Pass in the heart of Thornthwaite Forest and offering the very best of Lakeland hospitality. The mouth watering menus change each day, featuring a freshly prepared five course dinner thoughtfully planned to include some traditional local dishes, fresh vegetables and an irresistible selection of hot and cold English puddings. Bar meals and afternoon teas are also available. All bedrooms have hot drinks facilities, are centrally heated and most have private bath or shower. Owners Sandra and Barrie Littlefair look forward to welcoming all visitors.

QUARRY GARTH COUNTRY HOUSE HOTEL,
Troutbeck, Windermere,
Cumbria LA23 1LF

Tel: 096-62 3761

Residential licence; 11 bedrooms, all with private bathrooms; Children and dogs welcome; Car park (30); London 271 miles, Penrith 26, Kendal 8, Ambleside 5.

With spacious and comfortably-furnished rooms and delightful grounds of 8 acres, Quarry Garth offers excellent accommodation, food and service in the finest tradition of the English country house. Log fires and oak-panelling underline the warmth of welcome here and the guest rooms all have en suite facilities, central heating, colour television and tea and coffee-makers. Peacefully set on the eastern shores of Lake Windermere and only a short stroll from Brockhole National Trust Park, this pleasant haven has all the requirements for a Lakeland holiday to remember. Catering is first-class, the 30-seater restaurant offering Continental specialities as well as favourite British dishes.

Derbyshire

RIVERSIDE COUNTRY HOUSE HOTEL,
Ashford-in-the-Water, Bakewell,
Derbyshire

Tel: 062-981 4275

Licensed; 7 bedrooms, all with private bathrooms; Dogs by prior arrangement; Car park (27); Ashbourne 19 miles, Buxton 12.

A more delectable situation for a country hotel is hard to imagine. Hidden away in an unspoilt village between Bakewell and Buxton, the charming Riverside is certainly worth getting to know — not that the regular habitués who have already discovered this magical place will resent the intrusion. With elegant furnishings, oak-panelling and log fires burning in the inglenook fireplace, this splendid hotel, as its name implies, has an idyllic setting on the River Wye (good fishing) with the attractions of the Peak District National Park on all sides. Individually decorated bedrooms all have en suite facilities and tea and coffee-makers and the superb cuisine is memorable also for its presentation and imagination.

BIGGIN HALL,
Biggin-by-Hartington, Buxton,
Derbyshire SK17 0DH

Tel: 029-884 451

Restaurant and residential licence; 14 bedrooms, 11 with private bathrooms; Historic interest; Children welcome; Car park; Manchester 21 miles.

Biggin Hill is an historic house of 17th century origin, centrally situated in the Peak District National Park. It stands in its own spacious grounds of eight acres and has been completely renovated, whilst keeping the character of the Hall. The rooms are spacious and individually furnished with antiques. Visitors have a choice of two sitting rooms, one with colour television, the other with a large open stone fireplace. A good selection of wines complement the traditional farmhouse fare, rich in free range wholefoods and natural flavours.

THE CROFT COUNTRY HOUSE,
Great Longstone, Bakewell, Derbyshire

Tel: 062987 278*

Residential and restaurant licence; 8 bedrooms including Honeymoon Suite, 5 with private bathrooms/showers; Children welcome; Car park (25); Buxton 11 miles, Bakewell 3.

The galleried main hall from which all the bedrooms lead off, is a striking feature of The Croft, an attractive house of character set in its own 4-acre grounds. A lift has been thoughtfully provided for the less able. The busy restaurant serves an excellent menu with an impressive wine list. Apart from 2/3 weeks in February, The Croft is open all year and is an ideal centre for exploring the dramatic natural beauty of the Peak District. Historical interest is also well-served since Haddon Hall and the magnificent Chatsworth House are close by. Bakewell is a charming and busy market town. Buxton and Matlock are of course a short drive away.

PRIEST HOUSE HOTEL,
Kings Mills, Castle Donington, Derbyshire DE7 2RR

Tel: 0332 810649

Licensed; 14 bedrooms, all with private bathrooms; Historic interest; Children and dogs welcome; Car park (100); Leicester 23 miles, Derby 10.

This is an unusual venue for a holiday in the Midlands. The house itself was originally a water-mill mentioned in the Domesday Book, later turned into a mint in the reign of King James I, the site of a Cromwellian battle and a chapel where John Wesley once preached. Today, it is a most appealing country hotel, with guest rooms beautifully converted from seventeenth century mill-workers' cottages. Original features, including fireplaces and oak beams, have been retained, blending with such modern amenities as private bathrooms in the bedrooms along with colour television, radio, telephone, baby-listening devices and tea and coffee-making facilities. The lounge and bar are both attractively appointed, the restaurant offers a tempting selection of traditional fare and the handsome Riverside Suite caters for functions for up to 120 people. The River Trent's proximity means that there are opportunities for fishing and canoeing and, being centrally situated with easy access by road, rail and air, the hotel is popular for business meetings with two well-equipped seminar rooms set aside for this purpose.

Devon

DARTMOOR MOTEL,
Peartree Cross, Ashburton,
Devon TQ13 7JW

Tel: 0364 52232

Licensed; 28 bedrooms, all with private bathrooms or showers; 2 four poster honeymoon suites; Children and dogs welcome; Car park (50), garages (2); London 187 miles, Plymouth 24, Dartmouth 22, Exeter 20, Torquay 14, Newton Abbot 7.

Conveniently placed for all the numerous pleasures of South Devon, the motel lies midway between Exeter and Plymouth (leaving the A38 by signposting Two Bridges/Dartmoor, motel is 400 yards from junction) and is well known for its magnificent accommodation, with television, radio, baby listening, tea and coffee-making facilities and telephones provided in guest rooms from which there are open country views. Two bedrooms have four posters, and one has a jacuzzi bath. This free house has a luxurious lounge bar, and there is a high standard of cuisine in the restaurant, open to non-residents from 8am to 10pm. Central heating is installed throughout. The unfettered delights of Dartmoor are near at hand and one may enjoy salmon fishing and pony trekking in the immediate vicinity. *ETB* 🌸 🌸 🌸.

Please mention
Recommended COUNTRY HOTELS
when seeking refreshment or
accommodation at a Hotel
mentioned in these pages

BOVEY HOUSE HOTEL,
Beer, Seaton,
Devon EX12 3AD

Tel: 029-780 241*

Restaurant and residential licence; 12 bedrooms, 7 with private bathrooms; Historic interest; Children and dogs welcome; Car park (50); London 158 miles, Exeter 22, Sidmouth 9.

Of considerable historic interest, this sixteenth century manor house has been beautifully converted to serve the needs of modern day guests, yet retains many ancient features. In three acres of peaceful grounds, the house is approached down a tree-lined drive and immediately one enters the panelled Jacobean reception area one is captivated by the aura of a hallowed past. The oldest part is the present drawing room, once the medieval hall, and the adjacent Inglenooks Bar has a huge fifteenth-century fireplace. The superb dining room sets the scene for the delicious à la carte and table d'hôte cuisine. *Ashley Courtenay Recommended.*

PORTLEDGE HOTEL,
Fairy Cross, Bideford,
Devon EX39 5BX

Tel: 023-75 262

Licensed; 26 bedrooms, all with private bathrooms; Historic interest; Children welcome; Car park (50); Barnstaple 9 miles.

Reached by a long drive through oak and beech woods, the famous old manor house dates back to 1254. Retaining many fascinating historical features which recall days of opulence and prosperity, the house is now a magnificent country hotel with a large galleried lounge and guest rooms that are the last word in comfort. The dining room, with its superb ornamental ceiling, creates just the right atmosphere for memorable dining. The house is set in 60 acres of beautiful parkland and with its own bathing beach and there are opportunities for playing tennis, mini-golf and croquet as well as swimming in the heated pool or strolling along coastal and woodland paths.

BRACKEN HOUSE COUNTRY HOTEL,
Bratton Fleming, Barnstaple,
North Devon EX31 4TG

Tel: 05988 320

Licensed; 8 bedrooms, all with private bathrooms; Children over 12 welcome and dogs by special arrangement; Car park (12); Ilfracombe 15 miles, Lynton 13, Barnstaple 7.

Built as a rectory in 1840, this country hotel is rurally situated in eight acres with tennis court, croquet lawn and magnificent views. On the fringe of Exmoor, within easy reach of the glorious North Devon coast, the area provides a host of outdoor activities while the nearby Barnstaple Leisure Centre offers a wide range of indoor sports. The house is centrally heated throughout and has log fires in the public rooms. All bedrooms (including two ground-floor and two family suites) have private bathroom, tea/coffee facilities and colour TV. Relax in the two comfortable sitting rooms or make use of the large selection of books, jigsaws and games. A full English breakfast is offered and the three-course dinner menu, changed daily, is complemented by a good wine list. Vegetarian and special diets are catered for. Weekend breaks available all year together with special Christmas and New Year packages. Access and Visa accepted. *Ashley Courtenay Recommended.*

BOSSELL HOUSE HOTEL,
Plymouth Road, Buckfastleigh,
Devon TQ11 0DG

Tel: 0364-43294/43573

Residential and restaurant licence; 17 bedrooms, 6 with private bathrooms; Car park (30); Plymouth 21 miles, Kingsbridge 16, Totnes 6, Ashburton 3.

With its own parklike grounds of three acres, this charming country house hotel is a convenient place in which to stay, situated half way between Plymouth and Exeter. A variety of beaches may be reached within half-an-hour's drive and nearer at hand is the breathtaking scenery of Dartmoor. Buckfastleigh is interesting, with the butterfly farm and the terminus of the Dart Valley Railway. A trip on a steam train through verdant Devon countryside is to be recommended as is a visit to nearby Buckfast Abbey. As a holiday headquarters, Bossell House has all the requisites and more for guests of all ages. All rooms have colour television, telephone, and tea and coffee making facilities. A licensed, family run hotel which offers international cuisine prepared by the proprietor chef.

TIDWELL HOUSE COUNTRY HOTEL,
Knowle, Budleigh Salterton,
Devon EX9 7AG   Tel: 039-54 2444*

Restaurant and residential licence; 9 bedrooms, 7 with private bathrooms; Historic interest; Children and dogs welcome; Car park (20); Exmouth 4 miles.

Tall, square and delightfully Georgian, this old manor house retains the grace and elegance of its years, yet provides up-to-date amenities that will enchant the most obdurate guest. The warm and hospitable atmosphere has a great deal to do with this happy frame of mind. The house is surrounded by 4 acres of grounds and is only one mile from the sea, a peaceful setting that will soon restore jaded nerves. Jaded appetites will also be resuscitated by really excellent home cooking, meals being served in a spacious and attractive dining room or in Bertie's Cellar Restaurant which is also available to guests as a bar.

GIDLEIGH PARK,
Chagford,
Devon TQ13 8HH   Tel: 064-73 2367/2225

Residential and restaurant licence; 14 bedrooms, all with private bathrooms; Children and dogs welcome by arrangement; Car park; Bristol 79 miles, Exeter 15, Moretonhampstead 4.

1½ miles from the nearest road and hidden away in 30 acres of garden and woodland on the banks of the North Teign River, this peerless country hotel can fairly claim to be in 'deepest Devon'; certainly it is one of the most secluded in Britain. With a warm and welcoming atmosphere, this charming retreat conveys to visitors the feeling that they are honoured guests at a private country house party. Open log fires burn cheerfully throughout the year, fresh flowers abound and the superb bedrooms are individually furnished with exquisite taste, all having private bathroom, telephone and colour television. Most of them overlook the Teign Valley and, indeed, the views from the hotel are spectacular. In the hands of an expert chef, the cuisine is exceptional and backed by an astounding range of no less than 400 good wines. Situated in the quiet and lovely grounds are two croquet lawns, an all-weather tennis court and delightful water gardens. As the venue for a tranquil and rewarding country holiday within easy reach of Dartmoor and the sea, this fine hotel is recommended without reserve.

PLEASE ENCLOSE A STAMPED
ADDRESSED ENVELOPE WHEN
WRITING TO ENQUIRE ABOUT
ACCOMMODATION FEATURED IN
THIS GUIDE

EASTON COURT HOTEL,
Easton Cross, Chagford,
Devon TQ13 8JL

Tel: 064-73 3469

Residential and restaurant licence; 8 bedrooms, all with private bathrooms; Historic interest; Children over 14, dogs by arrangement; Car park (15); Exeter 20 miles, Okehampton 11.

This small, thatched Tudor house has a warm and welcoming ambience to cheer the seeker after tranquillity and relaxed comfort. From this peaceful holiday retreat of character one may savour the pleasures of adjacent Dartmoor as well as the varied seaside attractions of both north and south Devon coasts. The limited accommodation is beautifully set out with each guest room having its own private facilities. There is a sittingroom, bar and a library with log fires to brighten up chillier days. The restaurant, which is open to non-residents, provides first-class food which features local produce in some prominence. There is a good golf course nearby and facilities for riding and fishing.

RADFORDS COUNTRY HOTEL,
Lower Dawlish Water, Dawlish,
Devon EX7 0QN

Tel: 0626 863322*

Residential licence; 24 bedrooms, all with private bathrooms; Historic interest; Children and dogs welcome; Car park (40); Exeter 13 miles, Torquay 12, Newton Abbot 9, Teignmouth 3.

Holiday fun for guests of all ages in a glorious setting! 'Radfords' stands in six acres of grounds through which runs a stream on its way to the sea-front. Here, youngsters may play in safety and there is also a variety of playground equipment. An indoor swimming pool complex and an outdoor badminton court prove popular. Janet and Terry Crump, the proprietors, provide every facility for young children; entertainments are organised throughout the week, baby-sitters are provided and early teas are available on request. Adults, too, will be well pleased at the opportunities to relax in bar, games room and television lounge. Terry Crump is a qualified chef and the tempting cuisine is presented with obvious flair. The seaside fascinations of Dawlish are within strolling distance with sporting facilities in plenty close at hand. *1988 Peaudouce Award winners.*

LORD HALDON HOTEL,
Dunchideock, Near Exeter,
Devon EX6 7YF

Tel: 0392 832483

Licensed; 26 bedrooms, all with private bathrooms; Historic interest; Children and dogs welcome; Car park; 5 miles M5 Exit 31, Exeter 4 miles.

Built in 1720 as the seat of the Lords of Haldon the only surviving wing was part of one of Devon's largest and finest eighteenth century mansions. The Lord Haldon Hotel, with its excellent reputation for good food, accommodation, including a honeymoon suite, and interesting history, attracts visitors the world over. Here in restful surroundings with panoramic views where once stood the graceful marble halls of a bygone era, one can enjoy dinner in the candlelit restaurant. In the tranquillity of the gardens or in the cobbled courtyard, graced with its impressive Adam arch, one can enjoy delicious Devon cream teas, snacks and drinks alfresco. Dinner dances are held most Saturdays. *RAC***. ETB* 🌷 🌷 🌷 🌷.

SALSTON HOTEL,
Ottery St. Mary, Near Exeter,
Devon EX11 1RQ

Tel: 040-481 5581

Licensed; 27 bedrooms, all with private bathrooms; Historic interest; Children and dogs welcome; Car park (100); London 160 miles, Exeter 12, Honiton 6, Sidmouth 6.

Once the home of the Coleridge family, this lovely old manor house is set amidst superb Devon countryside and, today, offers fine holiday facilities for every member of the family. Private and public rooms are elegantly furnished and equipped with all modern comforts; all guest rooms have colour television, radio, direct dial telephone and baby-listening devices. Adventure playground for children, putting and croquet, plus an indoor heated swimming pool, sauna, mini-gymnasium, squash courts and sunbed. Excellent à la carte meals are served in the Otter View restaurant. Six golf courses and trout river nearby.

NOTE

All the information in this book is given in good faith in the belief that it is correct. However, the publishers cannot guarantee the facts given in these pages, neither are they responsible for changes in policy, ownership or terms that may take place after the date of going to press. Readers should always satisfy themselves that the facilities they require are available and that the terms, if quoted, still apply.

ALSTON HALL,
Battisborough Cross, Holbeton,
Near Plymouth, Devon PL8 1HN

Tel: 075-530 259

Licensed; 9 bedrooms, all with private bathrooms; Children welcome; Car park; Bristol 110 miles, Plymouth 10, Yealmpton 3.

The elegant opulence of the Edwardian era is a major attraction of this magnificent house which was skilfully converted into an hotel in 1960. One cannot but be impressed by the rich panelling in the Great Hall with its minstrels' gallery and the stained glass windows. This evidence of graceful luxury is carried on through the bar and lovely drawing room, the windows of which overlook the swimming pool to the sea beyond. Individually furnished and spacious, guest rooms are made for easy relaxation; each has a private bathroom, remote-control colour television, radio and direct-dial telephone. Table d'hôte and à la carte menus featuring traditional English and French cuisine will make mealtimes the subject of eager anticipation. With cliffs and sandy beaches close by on one hand and Dartmoor on the other, Alston Hall revels in a situation of outstanding natural beauty with the many pleasures of the fine city of Plymouth within easy reach. For the active, there are all-weather tennis courts within the 4½ acres of park-like grounds and golf at Bigbury is but a short distance away. Although grand, in the true sense, the hotel exudes a friendly atmosphere whilst maintaining the highest standards of service.

THE BELFRY,
Yarcombe, Honiton,
Devon EX14 9BD
Tel: 040-486 234/588

Restaurant and residential licence; 6 bedrooms, all with private bathrooms; Historic interest; Children over 12 years welcome; Car park (10); Honiton 6 miles.

The Belfry is a licensed, family run hotel which offers all the facilities required for a relaxing stay in the heart of some of the most beautiful countryside to be found in England. The hotel is centrally heated throughout and all the bedrooms have private bathrooms with colour television sets, direct dial telephone, hospitality trays and truly magnificent views of the river Yarty. The Belfry is ideally situated to explore the charms of East Devon, Somerset and Dorset.

BUCKLAND-TOUT-SAINTS HOTEL,
Goveton, Kingsbridge,
Devon TQ7 2DS
Tel: 0548 3055

Restaurant and residential licence; 12 bedrooms, all with private bathrooms; Historic interest; Children over 8 years welcome; Car park (20); Dartmouth 16 miles.

In the depths of the verdant South Devon countryside, this lovely Queen Anne house maintains the high tradition of lavish country estate entertaining of former days. The gracious manor house was built in 1690 and now, under the auspices of the Shephard family and their caring and efficient staff, the house plays host to discerning holidaymakers seeking tranquillity and the highest possible standards of comfort, cuisine and amenities in an elegant but informal atmosphere. Within easy reach of the coast, Dartmoor and many places of historical and sporting interest, Buckland-Tout-Saints stands in 27 acres of parkland which incorporates a croquet lawn and putting green, whilst bird watching, golf, riding, fishing and shooting may be arranged by prior notice. The de luxe rooms and suites on the main floor and the Buckland Room, with its hand-carved four-poster bed and antique furniture, represent the ultimate in graceful style. Each of the bedrooms is individually decorated and has a private bathroom, colour television, direct-dial telephone and other thoughtful extras. With luncheons and dinners also available to non-residents, beautifully presented meals in the modern British idiom, exhibiting originality and expertise, are served in the richly-panelled Queen Anne Restaurant with an extensive range of wines in support. Superb facilities are on hand for business meetings.

RECOMMENDED SHORT-BREAK HOLIDAYS
IN BRITAIN

Introduced by John Carter, TV Holiday Expert and Journalist

Specifically designed to cater for the most rapidly growing sector of the holiday market in the UK. Illustrated details of hotels offering special 'Bargain Breaks' throughout the year.

Available from newsagents and bookshops or direct from the publishers:
£2.95 plus 30p postage.

FHG PUBLICATIONS LTD
Abbey Mill Business Centre, Seedhill,
Paisley, Renfrewshire PA1 1JN

LEE MANOR COUNTRY HOUSE HOTEL
Lee Bay, North Devon EX34 8LR

Tel: 0271 63920

Residential and restaurant licence; 11 bedrooms, all with private bathroom and shower; Car park (15); Barnstaple 12 miles, Exmoor 14, Tiverton (M5) 42.

Lee Manor was built by a descendant of Sir Francis Drake in the Elizabethan style with magnificent oak beams, carved staircase and minstrel gallery around the Great Hall which is further enhanced by a huge log fire, gleaming brassware and candlelit tables to create a romantic and convivial atmosphere in which to dine from either an extensive à la carte or all inclusive table d'hôte menu which changes daily to include locally caught fish, fresh vegetables, home made soups and sweets. Comfortable lounges invite an evening's relaxation after a satisfying meal and a perfect night is assured in individually furnished fully en suite bedrooms with colour television, coffee/tea making, heating, etc. From a secluded hillside setting in its own 40 acres of wooded valley with long driveway leading down to the sea, Lee Manor has superb views overlooking the bay and unspoilt village of Lee where one can enjoy woodland walks or explore North Devon's awe inspiring coastline. Within easy reach are many attractive coastal towns, inland villages and the scenic beauty of Exmoor — in fact, an area which abounds with rural charm to provide an idyllic setting in which to enjoy the friendly atmosphere of Lee Manor whilst relaxing amidst its peace and tranquillity. Brochure forwarded on request.

LYDFORD HOUSE HOTEL,
Lydford, Okehampton, Devon EX20 4AU

Tel: 082-282 347

Licensed; 13 bedrooms, all with private bathrooms; Children over 5 and dogs welcome; Car park (30); Exeter 33 miles, Plymouth 25.

On the fringe of Dartmoor, this splendid and solid early-Victorian house has for some years been in the capable and caring hands of the Boulter family who have wrought many improvements in their time here to make this one of the finest country hotels in the West Country. Centrally heated throughout, the hotel has delightful guest rooms, each of which has colour television, radio and tea and coffee-making facilities and all have private bathrooms and WC's. Food here is a high priority, the day starting with a full English breakfast and concluding with a superb table d'hôte dinner with a wide choice at each course. Bar meals are available at lunchtime during the summer months. There is a comfortable lounge bedecked with water-colours of Dartmoor scenes, where a log fire burns merrily in winter and also a cosy cocktail bar with lounge adjoining. All around, the grandeur of Dartmoor beckons and riding, fishing and golfing enthusiasts are well catered for. Horse lovers, in fact, have no further to look than the hotel itself for the well-run stables in the grounds of 8 acres serve riders of all ages and all abilities. There is an all-weather school and tuition is available. Inclusive riding holidays are offered for the entire family at reasonable rates. The hotel has fishing rights over half-a-mile of the river Lyd, and residents will enjoy a discount off green fees when they play golf at Okehampton course.

HEWITT'S HOTEL,
North Walk, Lynton,
Devon EX35 6HJ

Tel: 0598 52293

Licensed; 12 bedrooms, 10 with private bathrooms; Historic interest; Children and dogs welcome; Car park (12); Ilfracombe 19 miles.

A private home in Victorian times, Hewitt's is of unusual architectural design. Now converted into a fine country house hotel, it is of great appeal to those seeking comfort, tranquillity and good living in delightful surroundings. Approached via a long drive, this homely retreat nestles in 27 acres of wooded grounds with the magnificent scenery of the North Devon coast and Exmoor National Park on the very doorstep. The hotel has a terrace with breathtaking views across the bay and there is an imposing panelled hall, a comfortable lounge and beautiful oak-panelled bar where a fire burns in cool weather. Bedrooms are large and appointed with private bath or shower, central heating, colour television, radio and direct-dial telephone. Many thoughtful extras are provided and some of the de-luxe rooms have balconies. Food is a priority at Hewitt's and the restaurant is acclaimed as the best in the area. Under the supervision of David Lamprell, a young and talented chef, the style of the cuisine is English with a French influence and there is an extensive selection of wines to complement each splendid dish. Children are very welcome and under 5's are accommodated free of charge in family rooms with meals charged as taken. A children's menu, cots and baby-listening facilities are available.

THE CROWN HOTEL,
Sinai Hill, Lynton,
Devon EX35 6AG

Tel: 0598 52253*

Licensed; 17 bedrooms, all with private bathrooms; Historic interest; Children and dogs welcome; Car park; London 202 miles, Barnstaple 20, Ilfracombe 19.

A place of rest and refreshment since 1760, this most attractive former coaching inn is now one of the foremost hotels on the North Devon coast. Diligent proprietors Alan and Thelma Westgarth go out of their way to ensure the comfort of all their guests. Bedrooms, all en suite, are attractively furnished, and each has colour TV, tea/coffee making facilities, radio/alarm, and direct-dial telephone. In a hotel where the emphasis is on friendly, personal service and customer satisfaction, great attention is naturally given to good food, with a fine table d'hôte selection and à la carte offering the best of local seafood and fresh vegetables whenever possible. Good real ale is also available in the cosy lounge. *AA**, RAC**.*

COMBE PARK HOTEL,
Hillsford Bridge, Near Lynton,
North Devon EX35 6LE

Tel: 0598 52356*

Restaurant and residential licence; 9 bedrooms, all with private bathrooms; Historic interest; Children over 12 years and dogs welcome; Car park; Ilfracombe 19 miles.

This former hunting lodge turned hotel enjoys an idyllic location in the centre of the National Trust Watersmeet Estate and just over two miles from the twin resorts of Lynton and Lynmouth. Set in grounds of 4½ acres through which flows the Hoar Oak Water, this tranquil and interesting retreat offers well-appointed guest rooms, all with private facilities; there are two attractive lounges and a comfortable bar for residents, whilst an excellent range of traditional dishes is served in a pleasant dining room. Opportunities for fishing and riding exist nearby and guests are cordially invited to bring along their dogs to further their enjoyment of the many beautiful walks in the area.

THE OLD RECTORY,
Martinhoe, Parracombe,
Devon

Tel: 059-83 368*

Table licence; 10 bedrooms, 9 with private bathrooms; Older children (12+), dogs by arrangement; Car park (14); Barnstaple 18 miles, Ilfracombe 13, Lynmouth 5.

Having just won the AA's coveted HBL merit award for the seventh successive year, the Old Rectory is firmly established as a small but select haven of peace and quiet. Surrounded by gardens with a lake, stream and putting green, this attractive Georgian house offers most bedrooms en suite with individual decoration and furnishing. The resident proprietors, Tony and Elizabeth Pring, maintain a high standard of cuisine, prepared and cooked by themselves. Relax in comfort after walks amid splendid scenery or the healthy efforts of horse-riding, fishing or golf which are all nearby. A colour brochure sent on request.

GLEBE HOUSE HOTEL,
North Bovey, Near Moreton Hampstead,
Devon TQ13 8RA

Tel: 0647 40544/40398

Residential licence; 9 bedrooms, 4 with private shower; Historic interest; Children and dogs welcome; Car park (30); Exeter 24 miles, Torquay 6.

Sheltered by its own 10 acres of woods, fields and gardens, this was once the local vicarage. Now offering the attractive combination of traditional hospitality and international cuisine, this is an enchanting little place in the heart of Devon with a quiet and unassuming atmosphere that will satisfy the need to relax and escape from urban pressures. Accommodation is of high standard and terms for twin or double-bedded rooms with toilet, bath or shower are most reasonable. Chef/Proprietor Mr. Lou Manzi prepares the intriguing French, Italian and even Middle Eastern cooking with obvious expertise and loving care. Children are welcome and accepted free of charge when sharing their parents' room.

YEOLDON HOUSE HOTEL,
Durrant Lane, Northam, Near Bideford,
Devon EX39 2RL

Tel: 023-72 74400/76618

Licensed; 10 bedrooms, all with private bathrooms; children and dogs welcome; Car park (30); Bideford 2 miles.

Today performing its function as a country house hotel of some distinction, Yeoldon House was originally the residence of an opulent Victorian gentleman who was responsible for the lovely landscaped grounds. With magnificent views over the River Torridge towards open countryside, the hotel is beautifully furnished throughout and is ideally situated for relaxing holidays at all times of the year. Guest rooms represent the ultimate in luxury, each having its own bath/shower and WC en suite, colour television, radio, direct-dial telephone, tea and coffee-making facilities and many thoughtful extras. Neil and Janet Turner run this fine hotel with kindly efficiency with the cuisine worthy of special mention. Menus are changed daily to incorporate a wide selection of English and Continental dishes with home-made specialities featuring prominently; especially noteworthy being local salmon and pheasant. Demi-pension terms include three courses from the nightly five-course menu and on Sunday night there is a candlelit smorgasbord with an extensive choice of fish, meat and salad. Children are welcome and High Teas provided for them. The delights of the North Devon coast are at hand and there are many sporting facilities in the district. Special Anniversary and Golfing Breaks are organised throughout the year. *AA**, RAC***, Egon Ronay and Ashley Courtenay Recommended.*

COURT HOUSE HOTEL,
Newton Ferrers,
Plymouth, Devon
Tel: 0752 872324*

Licensed; 9 bedrooms, all with private bathrooms; Historic interest; Children over 8 years and dogs welcome; Car park; Bristol 110 miles, Plymouth 10, Yealmpton 3.

A willing and courteous staff is but one feature by which a visit to this lovely old manor house will long be remembered, for the kindliest attention is given to guests of all ages. Rooms are luxuriously appointed with en suite facilities, colour television, radio and tea and coffee-makers and the cuisine is of an exceptionally high standard. Food and accommodation apart, there are a number of thoughtful aids to enjoyment provided; these include a cocktail bar, comfortable lounge and crackling log fires in cooler weather. In the spacious, wooded grounds is a fine heated swimming pool. Surrounded by lush countryside, the hotel is close to the River Yealm and boating enthusiasts will be in their element here.

VENN OTTERY BARTON,
Venn Ottery, Ottery St. Mary,
Devon EX11 1RZ
Tel: 040-481 2733

Residential licence; 16 bedrooms, 11 with private bathrooms or showers; Historic interest; Children welcome, dogs by arrangement; Car park (16); Exeter 11 miles.

A sixteenth century atmosphere with oak beams and log fires in Tudor fireplaces combines with twentieth century comforts to give guests the best of both worlds at warm and welcoming Venn Ottery Barton. Formerly a farmhouse, the hotel proudly upholds the tradition of good country cooking, using plenty of fresh local produce. Admirably situated for exploring glorious Dartmoor, there is a wealth of castles, abbeys, country parks and popular coastal resorts within easy reach. And just imagine, too, after an active day and a delicious meal, the pleasure of relaxing in the comfortable lounge enjoying a drink from the bar or even trying one's skills in the games room! *ETB* 🌸🌸🌸*, Ashley Courtenay recommended, AA, RAC listed.*

SIDMOUNT HOTEL,
Station Road, Sidmouth,
Devon EX10 8XJ
Tel: 039-55 3432*

Residential and restaurant licence; 15 bedrooms, all with private bathrooms; Historic interest; Car park (16); Lyme Regis 17 miles, Exeter 15.

A fine Georgian hotel of character in a quiet position set in two acres of beautiful gardens which contain over 300 different varieties of trees and shrubs. The hotel commands superb sea and country views of the Devonshire landscape. All bedrooms have private bathrooms and are well equipped, with colour television, and tea and coffee making facilities. A central feature of the hotel is a splendid oak staircase, which leads to the bedrooms. The hotel offers a high standard of comfort and excellent food. Colour brochure available on request.

WOODY BAY HOTEL,
Woody Bay, Parracombe,
Devon EX31 4QX

Tel: 059-83 264*

Licensed; 14 bedrooms, 13 with private bathrooms; Children over 8 and well-behaved dogs welcome; Car park (15); Barnstaple 18 miles, Ilfracombe 13, Lynton and Lynmouth 5.

There can be few hotels enjoying such a spectacular situation as the Woody Bay, a fine late Victorian hotel, magnificently set amongst hundreds of trees, gazing across the Bristol Channel to the Welsh mountains beyond. The relaxing lounge, complete with log fire for cooler days (the hotel is centrally heated), offers games, pastimes and plenty of local information to help plan your holiday. A good and varied choice at all meals is the keynote of the attractive diningroom and the pretty patio with its little waterfall makes a delightful spot for an *al fresco* luncheon. *AA**, RAC**. Recommended by Egon Ronay, Ashley Courtenay and Relais Routiers.*

BROOKDALE COUNTRY HOUSE HOTEL,
North Huish, South Brent,
Devon

Tel: 054-882 402*

Residential and restaurant licence; 8 bedrooms, all with private bathrooms; Historic interest; Children over 10 welcome; Car park; Torquay 20 miles, Totnes 13, Buckfastleigh 8.

Winding woodland paths, a bubbling stream and a lovely waterfall are features of the four delightful acres and woods which surround this impressive country house. Surrounded by the peace of the lush Devon countryside, this old rectory has stood serene for over 150 years in a situation only three miles from Dartmoor and eight from the coast. Homeliness and warmth are immediately apparent on entering the house and guest rooms are spacious, beautifully furnished and well appointed, including colour television. Excellent meals featuring home produce are served in a charming dining room which is candlelit in the evening and restful moments may be sought in a large drawing room which has its own bar.

BOWDEN CLOSE HOTEL,
Teignmouth Road, Maidencombe, Torquay, Devon TQ1 4TJ
Tel: 0803 38029

Licensed; 19 bedrooms, 17 with private facilities; Children and pets welcome; Car park (25), garaging (2); Exeter 20 miles.

Delightful elevated Victorian country house midway between Torquay and Teignmouth with panoramic sea and coastal views. Friendly, informal atmosphere with emphasis on comfort, courtesy and good food. Ideal for walking, touring or just relaxing. Close to Torbay attractions without the hustle and bustle. 19 bedrooms, mostly en suite, all with colour television and tea making facilities. Central heating. Ample parking. Open all year. 600 yards from sheltered beach. Write or telephone for brochure. *AA**, RAC**, ETB* 🌹 🌹 🌹.

HIGHBULLEN HOTEL,
Chittlehamholt, Umberleigh, North Devon EX37 9HD
Tel: 076-94 561

Licensed; 35 bedrooms, all with private bathrooms; Historic interest; Children over 10 years welcome; Car park; Barnstaple 8 miles.

Perched in wooded seclusion between two valleys, this is a splendid Gothic mansion set in 60 acres of parkland in which deer roam and with a 9-hole golf course, all-weather tennis court, swimming pool and croquet lawn. Accommodation is magnificent, both in the main house and in the adjacent farm buildings which have been converted into luxury guest rooms; all have private bathroom and central heating. Friendly and informal, this is a lovely place where the accent is on comfort and excellent food. Quiet relaxation may be sought in the drawing room, conservatory, library and secluded corners of the grounds. Other attractions include indoor tennis courts and swimming pool, squash, billiards, sauna, jacuzzi, spa bath and sunbed. Massage and hairdressing available by arrangement.

> * The appearance of an asterisk after the telephone number indicates that the hotel in question is closed for a period during the winter months. Exact dates should be ascertained from the hotel itself.

WOOLACOMBE BAY HOTEL,
Woolacombe,
Devon EX34 7BN
Tel: 0271 870388*

Licensed; 48 bedrooms, all with private bathrooms; Children welcome; Car park (100); London 231 miles, Lynton 21, Ilfracombe 6.

'The Hedonist's Hotel' is the boast here, and any visitors with an appreciation of the good things in life and a wish to indulge themselves for a while will certainly not be disappointed. Set in the centre of the village in six acres of grounds running to three miles of clean, golden sands, the Woolacombe Bay Hotel must surely be everyone's idea of a dream holiday location. Public rooms are elegantly yet comfortably furnished, reflecting the hotel's traditions of style and fine service, while luxuriously furnished bedrooms and self contained suites, all with satellite television and video, offer a holiday choice to suit all visitors. Guests can linger at the hotel all day if they wish, for leisure facilities are superb, with disco, dancing, squash, solarium, spa bath, billiards, aerobics, an indoor pool, and children's sports organiser. The pleasures of good food are given serious consideration, too, in the hotel's sumptuous five-course breakfast and seven-course dinner menus. Fine wine chosen from a substantial selection will complement your meal. *AA***, RAC***, ETB* 🌸 🌸 🌸.

PRINCE HALL HOTEL,
Two Bridges, Yelverton,
Devon PL20 6SW
Tel: 082-289 403

Restaurant and residential licence; 8 bedrooms, all with private bathrooms; Historic interest; Children and dogs welcome; Car park (20); Plymouth 10 miles.

The Prince Hall Hotel is a small, friendly and relaxed country house hotel, in a peaceful and secluded setting, commanding glorious views over open moorland. All bedrooms are en suite, some with four poster beds. The hotel offers log fires, excellent cuisine and personal service, and is ideally situated for wonderful walking, riding and fishing. *ETB* 🌸 🌸 🌸 🌸

Dorset

YALBURY COTTAGE,
**Lower Bockhampton, Dorchester,
Dorset DT2 8PZ**

Tel: 0305 62382

*Restaurant licence; 8 bedrooms, all with private facilities; Historic interest; Car park (19);
Dorchester 2 miles.*

This thatched cottage in Thomas Hardy's 'Mellstock' is the perfect country house location for exploring Dorset with its many and varied places of interest. For lovers of literature, Yalbury is midway between Hardy's birthplace at Higher Bockhampton and his final resting-place at Stinsford Church. Enjoy the comfortable charm of beams and inglenook fireplaces after country walks, riding, fishing or golf nearby and visits to the historical county town of Dorchester. The recently completed bedrooms, double and twin, are all en suite, with colour television, radio and tea/coffee-making facilities. The well-established Yalbury Cottage Restaurant's à la carte cusine offers gourmet dining at special inclusive residents' prices and Wine Tastings are a special feature.

MAIDEN NEWTON HOUSE,
**Maiden Newton, Near Dorchester,
Dorset DT2 0AA**

Tel: 0300 20336*

*Residential and restaurant licence; 6 bedrooms, all with private bathrooms; Historic interest;
Children and dogs welcome; Car park (15); Dorchester 8 miles.*

A grand old manor house in a classic English village, Maiden Newton House dates back to the 15th century although it was substantially rebuilt 400 years later. With a warmth of welcome epitomised by mellow stonework, mullioned windows and soaring chimneys, the house, standing in 21 acres of parkland and gardens, represents country house living at its best. Enlightened Proprietors Elizabeth and Bryan Ferris have decorated each suite and guest room in distinctive and individual style. All are sumptuously appointed and have their own private bathrooms. Ornaments, paintings and books induce a feeling of genteel relaxation substantiated, in practical fashion, by the delectable cuisine with seafood a speciality. The hotel will appeal to anglers for ¾-mile of private trout water is available to guests.

NOTE

All the information in this book is given in good faith in the belief that it is correct. However, the publishers cannot guarantee the facts given in these pages, neither are they responsible for changes in policy, ownership or terms that may take place after the date of going to press. Readers should always satisfy themselves that the facilities they require are available and that the terms, if quoted, still apply.

MILTON MANOR HOTEL,
Milton Abbas, Blandford Forum, Dorset

Tel: 0258 880254*

Residential licence; 12 bedrooms, 10 with private bathrooms; Historic interest; Car park (20); Bournemouth 23 miles, Dorchester 11.

Far from the madding crowd this fine old country hotel in Hardy Country may be but guests may be assured of the most modern appointments in their search for the ultimate in peaceful relaxation. The house stands in its own 7 acres of wooded grounds and the surrounding Dorset countryside hides many delectable beauty spots. It is only a short stroll to the delightful thatched village of Milton Abbas with its fourteenth century abbey and the lovely beaches of the Purbeck coast are within easy reach. Hearty appetites will be well satisfied by the excellent cuisine, much of the produce being home grown. A putting green and croquet lawn may engender a spirit of friendly competition before repairing to the cosy residents' bar.

KNOLL HOUSE HOTEL,
Studland, Near Swanage, Dorset BH19 3AH

Tel: 092-944 251

Restaurant and residential licence; 80 bedrooms, 56 with private bathrooms, including 30 family suites; Children and dogs welcome; Car park (100); Corfe Castle 6 miles, Sandbanks Ferry 3.

On the Dorset Heritage coast this delightful hotel is surrounded by National Trust land and some of the prettiest scenery in the West Country. Knoll House is an independent country house hotel under the personal management of its owners. It overlooks three miles of beach from an attractive setting in pine trees and pleasant gardens and offers facilities for sport and relaxation that must be counted amongst the finest in the country — two hard tennis courts, a pitch and putt course and a swimming pool. The Health Spa offers a sauna, steam-room, Jacuzzi and other leisure pursuits. Young children are catered for in their own diningroom.

FISHERMAN'S HAUNT HOTEL,
Winkton, Christchurch, Dorset BH23 7AS

Tel: 0202 477283/484071

Licensed; 19 bedrooms, all with private shower/bathrooms; Historic interest; Children and dogs welcome; Car park (100); Christchurch 2 miles.

By the banks of the meandering Avon and surrounded by the beauties of the New Forest, this lovely old country house beckons country lovers and anglers in particular. Although dating back to 1673, the house now provides the most modern facilities and attractive furnishings throughout. Under the auspices of resident proprietor James Bochan, the hotel presents a high standard of cuisine and wines. Excellent luncheons and dinners are served in the river-view restaurant. Guest rooms are delightfully furnished and all are centrally heated and have colour television and tea and coffee-making facilities; some are available with four poster beds. There are two bars serving traditional ales and snacks. Coarse fishing in the Avon provides first-rate sport and for golfers there are several courses within easy reach. *House of Hospitality Awards, AA, RAC, ETB* 🌷 🌷 🌷 🌷.

KEMPS COUNTRY HOUSE HOTEL,
East Stoke, Wareham,
Dorset BH20 6AL

Tel: 0929 462563

Residential licence; 9 bedrooms, 8 with private bathrooms; Children welcome; Historic interest; Car park (26); Dorchester 17 miles, Poole 10.

A friendly welcome can be expected at Kemps Country House Hotel and Restaurant. The hotel is set in unspoilt Dorset countryside overlooking the Frome Valley. Originally a Victorian Rectory, the house has been tastefully extended and the interior elegantly preserved. All rooms are tastefully decorated and have television, direct-dial telephone and tea and coffee making facilities. Kemps' restaurant is renowned for its quality and originality, all the food is freshly produced from local produce, where possible, and bread is baked twice daily. Wines are constantly being added to the comprehensive wine list. Local amenities include golf courses, tennis, fishing, riding and sailing.

STOCK HILL HOUSE HOTEL,
Wyke, Gillingham,
Dorset SP8 5NR

Tel: 074-76 3626*

Residential and restaurant licence; 6 bedrooms, all with private facilities; Historic interest; Children over 7 years welcome; Car park; Bristol 46 miles, Bournemouth 34.

In tranquil Dorset countryside, the beautifully-restored early Victorian manor house stands in 10 acres of parkland and woods and is approached down a long drive flanked by graceful beech trees. In this idyllic rural setting, one will soon relax and enjoy the hospitality, comfort and excellent food provided by Chef-Proprietor Peter Hauser and his wife, Nita. Log fires brighten up dull days and crystal chandeliers twinkle in the evenings, promoting convivial conversation. Sound repose will soon follow in guest rooms luxuriously appointed with bathroom/shower, colour television, radio, direct-dial telephone, hair dryer and trouser press. Ironing facilities. Popular diversion is provided by a heated indoor swimming pool and a croquet lawn.

Durham

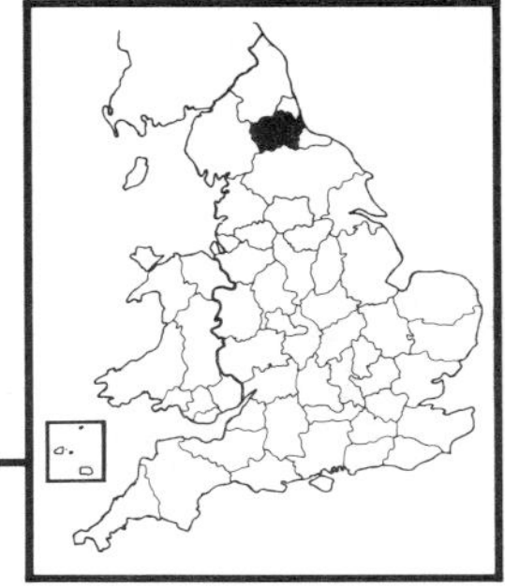

MORRITT ARMS HOTEL,
Rokeby, Near Barnard Castle,
Co. Durham
Tel: 0833 27232

Licensed; 23 bedrooms, 16 with private bathrooms; Historic interest; Children and dogs welcome; Car park (100), garages (3); London 248 miles, Richmond 11, Barnard Castle 4.

The proprietors of this fine hotel describe its setting as 'inconceivably perfect', and while acknowledging that they may be a little biased it is hard to disagree with them — especially as in doing so one would also be disagreeing with Sir Walter Scott who considered it 'one of the most enviable places I have ever seen'. The Morritt Arms offers all that one would expect of a good modern hotel: comfortable, well equipped bedrooms, tastefully furnished and relaxing public rooms, attentive service and a high standard of cuisine. A special play area is available for children. Short break holidays available. *Egon Ronay recommended.*

Essex

THE CROWN HOUSE,
Great Chesterford, Saffron Walden,
Essex CB10 1NY
Tel: 0799 30515/30257

Restaurant and residential licence; 18 bedrooms, all with private bathrooms; Historic interest; Children and dogs welcome by arrangement; Car park (30); Saffron Walden 4 miles.

Leaving the M11 and winding a short distance through cornfields to the delightful village of Great Chesterford, reminded us of the rural attractions of a relatively unconsidered part of England. On the edge of the village, waiting to provide discerning tourists with modern amenities of the highest order, the refurbished Crown House is a welcoming sight. Listed as being of architectural and historic interest, the hotel has superb guest rooms, all of which have private bathrooms, colour television and direct-dial telephones, whilst the imaginative and reasonably-priced cuisine, backed by wines to satisfy any connoisseur, is on all evidence more popular than ever. Conveniently near Cambridge and Newmarket, the hotel's beautifully panelled Georgian Room is in great demand for conferences and special functions.

Gloucestershire

BIBURY COURT HOTEL,
Bibury,
Gloucestershire GL7 5NT

Tel: 028-574 337

Licensed; 17 bedrooms, 16 with private bathrooms, including one suite; Historic interest; Children and dogs welcome; Car park (100); Cheltenham 17 miles, Stow-on-the-Wold 14, Burford 10, Cirencester 7.

With an atmosphere acquired by centuries of gracious living, Bibury Court offers tranquillity, relaxation and good living with a complete absence of formality. This beautiful and imposing mansion dates from Tudor times, although the main block was built in 1633. The home of the Sackville family for generations, the house has eight acres of grounds and a lovely setting beside the River Coln. Trout fishing is available and other sporting facilities nearby include golf and riding. Direct-dial telephones and colour television in all rooms. A fine base from which to tour the Cotswolds or visit Stratford, Oxford, Cheltenham and Bath, this great but warmly welcoming house provides accommodation, food and wine of high standing.

CHESTER HOUSE HOTEL AND MOTEL,
Bourton-on-the-Water,
Gloucestershire

Tel: 0451 20286

Restaurant and residential licence; 22 bedrooms, all with private bathrooms or showers; Children and dogs welcome; Car park (25); Gloucester 24 miles, Cheltenham 16, Cirencester 16.

This wholesome establishment is not a typical motel for its accommodation is in a converted row of old Cotswold stone stables. Guest rooms are sumptuously appointed, each having its own bathroom, phone, radio, intercom, central heating and colour television. The original hotel area comprises five garden suites and double and single rooms, all with bath or shower, as well as a cocktail bar and licensed restaurant where guests may enjoy first-class English cooking. The comfort of guests is the personal concern of proprietor, Julian Davies, and this charming hotel is an ideal touring base for the Cotswolds. *ETB* ♣ ♣ ♣.

COTSWOLD HOUSE HOTEL & RESTAURANT,
The Square, Chipping Campden,
Gloucestershire GL55 6AN

Tel: 0386 840330

Licensed; 15 bedrooms, all with private bathrooms; Historic interest; Children over 8 welcome; Car park (10); London 91 miles, Oxford 35, Stratford-upon-Avon 12.

This listed Regency building enjoys pride of place on Campden's historic High Street, once described as 'The most beautiful village street left in this island'. But the Cotswold House is unique not only for its lovely setting, but also for its standards of luxury and comfort. Each of the 15 bedrooms has an individual theme, and is sumptuously furnished, with themes ranging from Gothic through Indian to Military, offering an experience in themselves. Interestingly English cooking is served in the Restaurant, which enjoys an enviable reputation, and fine food is also served in the All-Day Eaterie. Cotswold House offers a unique accommodation experience to delight the most discerning of guests. *AA***, RAC***; ETB* 👑 👑 👑 👑.

FOR THE MUTUAL GUIDANCE
OF GUEST AND HOST

Every year literally thousands of holidays, short-breaks and overnight stops are arranged through our guides, the vast majority without any problems at all. In a handful of cases, however, difficulties do arise about bookings, which often could have been prevented from the outset.

It is important to remember that when accommodation has been booked, both parties — guests and hosts — have entered into a form of contract. We hope that the following points will provide helpful guidance.

GUESTS: When enquiring about accommodation, be as precise as possible. Give exact dates, numbers in your party and the ages of any children. State the number and type of rooms wanted and also what catering you require — bed and breakfast, full board, etc. Make sure that the position about evening meals is clear — and about pets, reductions for children or any other special points.

Read our reviews carefully to ensure that the proprietors you are going to contact can supply what you want. Ask for a letter confirming all arrangements, if possible.

If you have to cancel, do so as soon as possible. Proprietors do have the right to retain deposits and under certain circumstances to charge for cancelled holidays if adequate notice is not given and they cannot re-let the accommodation.

HOSTS: Give details about your facilities and about any special conditions. Explain your deposit system clearly and arrangements for cancellations, charges, etc, and whether or not your terms include VAT.

If for any reason you are unable to fulfil an agreed booking without adequate notice, you may be under an obligation to arrange alternative suitable accommodation or to make some form of compensation.

While every effort is made to ensure accuracy, we regret that FHG Publications cannot accept responsibility for errors, omissions or misrepresentation in our entries or any consequences thereof. Prices in particular should be checked because we go to press early. We will follow up complaints but cannot act as arbiters or agents for either party.

STRATTON HOUSE HOTEL,
Gloucester Road, Cirencester,
Gloucester GL7 2LE

Tel: 0285 61761

Licensed; 26 bedrooms, 23 with private bathrooms or shower; Historic interest; Children and dogs welcome; Car park (100); Stratford-on-Avon 41 miles, Oxford 36, Stow-on-the-Wold 19, Gloucester 17, Cheltenham 16, Stroud 12.

The first-time visitor to this unique hotel may be forgiven for thinking he had inadvertently entered a private country residence as every detail has received personal attention. Bedrooms are spacious and well appointed. The drawing room is delightfully furnished and contains many fine antiques and paintings. The superb restaurant is in three interconnecting sections each with a character of its own and, like the drawing room, opens on to gardens which are a joy from spring to late autumn. On cooler nights a crackling log fire is a welcome feature of the entrance hall and also the timbered bar where guests may enjoy a drink in comfort and style. Difficult though it may be to leave such a haven of tranquillity as Stratton House, some time must be given to a leisurely exploration of the surrounding area. Cirencester itself holds more of historic interest than can be mentioned here, and the beauty of the Cotswolds should need no description. *ETB* 🌹🌹🌹🌹.

CORINIUM COURT HOTEL,
12 Gloucester Street, Cirencester,
Gloucestershire GL7 2DG

Tel: 0285 69711

Licensed; 16 bedrooms, all with private bathrooms; Historic interest; Children and dogs welcome; Car park (40); Stroud 12 miles.

This most delightful hotel was built in 1595 as a wool merchant's house. Now beautifully transformed into an hotel offering a high standard of accommodation and food, Corinium Court is today blessed with guest rooms, all of which have colour television, radio, telephone, central heating and private facilities. Some are on the ground floor and are particularly suitable for disabled visitors. Converted from the old barn and wagon shed, the charming candlelit restaurant is the setting for fine chef-prepared food made even more pleasurable by attentive service. Other appealing features include the Courtyard Lounge Bar, originally the coach-house and the Austrian-style Alpine Room which overlooks a pretty walled garden.

NOTE

All the information in this book is given in good faith in the belief that it is correct. However, the publishers cannot guarantee the facts given in these pages, neither are they responsible for changes in policy, ownership or terms that may take place after the date of going to press. Readers should always satisfy themselves that the facilities they require are available and that the terms, if quoted, still apply.

LAMBSQUAY HOUSE HOTEL,
Near Coleford,
Gloucestershire GL16 8QB

Tel: 0594 33127

Licensed; 7 bedrooms, all with private bathrooms; Children and dogs welcome; Car park (30); Gloucester 19 miles, Chepstow 13.

For business or pleasure, this is a lovely retreat buried in the heart of the Royal Forest of Dean. Elegantly Georgian, the house is situated on the top of a hill and is closely surrounded by meadowland. Comfortable, warm and peaceful, the house has many attractive features, in particular the charming Victorian lounge/cocktail bar with its ornate ceiling, carved marble fireplace and delightful furnishings. The dining room overlooks the garden and ornamental pond; in this delightful room a first-rate table d'hôte menu will tempt the most jaded palate. Individually decorated guest rooms are equipped with colour television, radio and tea and coffee-making facilities and all have a bathroom en suite.

PAINSWICK HOTEL,
Kemps Lane, Painswick,
Gloucestershire GL6 6YB

Tel: 0452 812160

Residential and restaurant licence; 15 bedrooms, all with private bathrooms; Historic interest; Children and dogs welcome; Car park (25); Stroud 3 miles.

Widely recognised as being in the top echelon of establishments in the Cotswolds or, indeed, the West of England, this beautiful Georgian house has an imposing frontage that gives only a clue to the ambience of warmth, luxury and good living within, epitomised by the lounge with an open fire, convivial oak-panelled bar and the drawing room that overlooks the croquet lawn. Guest rooms are magnificently appointed with private bath/shower, colour television, radio, telephone and delightful views. The hotel maintains an extremely high standard of cuisine backed by efficient and friendly service, meals being served in a splendid panelled restaurant illuminated by crystal chandeliers.

FOSSE MANOR HOTEL,
Stow-on-the-Wold,
Gloucestershire
Tel: 0451 30354

Licensed; 20 double bedrooms, 16 with private bathrooms, 4 single; Children and dogs welcome; Car park (100); Oxford 27 miles, Stratford-upon-Avon 21, Cirencester 19, Cheltenham 18, Evesham 16, Burford 10.

Recently modernised, this is an hotel which combines the charm of a Cotswold manor house with the comforts and amenities demanded by the guest of today. The house is surrounded by pleasantly-wooded grounds and gardens with ample parking space. Bedrooms are well appointed and most have a private bathroom or shower en suite. Imaginative English and Continental cuisine is served in the Candlelight Room, accompanied by a well-chosen selection of wines. All rooms have colour television. There is also a conference room and a beauty salon.

WYCK HILL HOUSE HOTEL,
Stow-on-the-Wold,
Gloucestershire GL54 1HY
Tel: 0451 31936

Licensed; 23 bedrooms, all with private bathrooms; Historic interest; Children over six years welcome; Car park (60), garaging (4); Cheltenham 18 miles.

Amidst terraced lawns and woods, this imposing Cotswold manor house, built in mellow honey-coloured stone, lies well back from the road in its own landscaped gardens. Peace, panoramic views and proximity to numerous places of historic and sporting interest is only part of this fine hotel's attraction for the accommodation provided is magnificent. An impressive stairway rises from the Grand Hall to a galleried landing above: leading off are the bedrooms, all of which have private bath/shower, colour television, radio and telephone installed. Under the supervision of an expert chef, the bill of fare is very extensive and there is a comfortable bar and well-stocked cellar.

CALCOT MANOR,
Near Tetbury,
Gloucestershire GL8 8YJ
Tel: 066-689 355/227*

Restaurant and residential licence; 14 bedrooms, all with private bathrooms; Historic interest; Children over 12 years welcome; Car park (40); Cirencester 11 miles.

The lovely stone barns and stables of this former farmhouse include a 14th-century tithe barn which is one of the oldest in Britain. Now an enchanting country hotel in the heart of the Cotswolds, Calcot Manor offers quietude, delightful accommodation, excellent food and personal service. Although secluded, Bath, Cheltenham and many places of interest are conveniently near, whilst stay-at-homes may swim in the heated pool, play croquet or relax with a book in a leafy corner of the grounds with lunch served on the terrace. Dinner is more formal with dishes prepared by a gifted chef. Each bedroom has a private bathroom and is a joy in itself.

TWIGWORTH LODGE HOTEL,
Twigworth,
Gloucestershire GL2 9PG Tel: 0452 730266

Licensed; 27 bedrooms; Historic interest; Children and dogs welcome; Car park (80); London 106 miles, Cheltenham 8, Gloucester 3.

A superb Grade A listed Georgian building set in three acres of its own grounds, in the country but only a short distance from the beautiful cities of Gloucester and Cheltenham. Bedrooms are delightfully appointed, all being en suite and enjoying views of the surrounding grounds. À la carte meals are served in the delightful restaurant, and bar meals are also available for those who prefer lighter fare. There is an indoor heated pool for guests' use. Twigworth Lodge is a fine base from which to see the lovely Cotswolds countryside, and the Forest of Dean is also within easy reach. *ETB* 👑👑👑👑.

Hampshire

CAREYS MANOR HOTEL,
Brockenhurst, New Forest,
Hampshire Tel: 0590 23551

Licensed; 80 bedrooms, all with private bathrooms; Historic interest; Car park; Bournemouth 17 miles, Ringwood 11, Lymington 5, Lyndhurst 4.

The sweeping, flower-lined drive, the mellow brick of the old garden walls, the imposing entrance — all are evocative of a bygone age. This elegant privately-owned hotel is renowned for its consistently high standards of cuisine, comfort and service and has beautifully appointed bedrooms, some with four posters, offering a classic theme in the main building, whilst those in the Garden Wing (linked to the main building by a covered way) are modern, opening directly on to the lawn or having balconies which overlook the five acres of landscaped gardens. All bedrooms have colour television. The New Forest area is justifiably famed for its fine walks and riding, sailing and golf are also available. Careys Manor offers exceptional leisure facilities including swimming pool, jacuzzi, sauna, steam room, massage and beauty treatments and a supervised gymnasium where the full-time instructor will be happy to guide you in your personal fitness programme.

NEW PARK MANOR,
Brockenhurst, New Forest,
Hampshire
Tel: 0590 23467

Licensed; 27 bedrooms, all with private bathrooms; Historic interest; Children and dogs welcome; Car park (40); Lymington 5 miles.

Historical records indicate that this beautiful manor house dates back to the days of William the Conqueror and was, in later days, the favourite hunting lodge of King Charles. Though modernised, the old house still retains its original rooms with massive beams and open log fires, interesting carvings and superb fireplaces in which open fires burn in winter. All bedrooms have colour television and telephones. Some of the rooms have four posters. In the romantic atmosphere of the candlelit restaurant with its open log fire you will enjoy good food complemented by fine wines. Facilities include a fine outdoor heated swimming pool and tennis court. New Park Manor has its own stables to which guests are welcome to bring their own horses and dogs, and you can ride directly into the Forest and heathland from the hotel.

WHITLEY RIDGE COUNTRY HOUSE HOTEL,
Beaulieu Road, Brockenhurst,
Hampshire SO42 7QL
Tel: 0590 22354/22463

Residential and restaurant licence; 13 bedrooms, 11 with private bathrooms; Historic interest; Children and dogs welcome; Car park (30); Lyndhurst 4 miles.

Georgian in style, Whitley Ridge was built in the late 18th century as a Royal Hunting Lodge and was later extended in Victorian times. Much of the grace and form of those days remains despite recent improvements at the sympathetic hands of owners Rennie and Sue Law, who are supported by a friendly and attentive staff. Situated in lovely grounds of 5 acres incorporating a tennis court, this welcoming place is a veritable jewel set in the verdant heart of the New Forest. Refreshingly imaginative and reasonably-priced dishes are served in a delightful restaurant with a cosy bar and comfortable drawing room adjacent. Guest rooms are very well appointed and one with a four-poster bed is available. *ETB* 🌺 🌺 🌺 🌺.

THE COTTAGE HOTEL AND RESTAURANT,
Sway Road, Brockenhurst,
Hampshire SO42 7SH
Tel: 0590 22296

Restaurant licence; 6 bedrooms, all with private bathrooms; Historic interest; Car park (10), Bournemouth 18 miles, Southampton 13.

A delightfully converted New Forest cottage where guests receive a warm welcome and excellent service. All bedrooms are en suite, with colour television and tea makers. The oak-beamed lounge, with its cosy log fire in winter, ensures that guests can relax in comfort throughout the year. The Cottage is highly recommended and the proprietors' aim is to make sure that all guests have a restful holiday or break so, regretfully, no children or pets are accepted. *RAC Highly Acclaimed. ETB* 👑 👑 👑.

EVERGREENS HOTEL,
Romsey Road, Lyndhurst,
Hampshire SO43 7AR
Tel: 042-128 2175/2343

Residential and restaurant licence; 20 bedrooms, 18 with private shower/bathrooms; Historic interest; Children and dogs welcome; Car park; London 83 miles, Salisbury 19.

This country house hotel is situated in two acres of lovely garden close to the centre of Lyndhurst, capital of the New Forest. It is personally run by the Austrian proprietor/chef and guests can, therefore, expect good food and the best of attention to their requirements in a very friendly atmosphere. Amenities include bedrooms with private shower and toilet, colour television, telephone, tea/coffee facilities, sittingroom, a cosy bar with log fire and an outdoor heated swimming pool. A vegetable garden provides fresh produce for the restaurant and menus feature a variety of English and Continental dishes. Come and let us spoil you.

LITTLE FOREST LODGE,
Poulner Hill, Ringwood,
Hampshire
Tel: 0425 478848

Residential licence; 5 bedrooms, all with private bathrooms; Children welcome; Car park (10); London 95 miles, Southampton 20, Salisbury 17, Bournemouth 11.

A luxurious little hotel set in three acres of landscaped grounds one mile from Ringwood and in walking distance of the beautiful New Forest. Proprietors Jane and Eric Martin ensure that guests receive a warm welcome, with the highest standards of comfort and hospitality. All bedrooms are tastefully furnished with guests' comfort in mind, with en suite facilities, television, and individual decor. A full English breakfast is served in the wood panelled diningroom, and home cooking is good and plentiful. Children are welcome, and the baby listening service provided is just another of the Lodge's thoughtful touches. *AA, RAC.*

STRING OF HORSES,
Mead End, Sway, Lymington,
Hampshire SO41 6EH
Tel: 0590 682631

Residential licence; 6 bedrooms, all with private facilities; Car park (20); Bournemouth 15; Southampton 15 miles.

Unique secluded exclusive hotel set in four acres in the heart of the New Forest, with a friendly, relaxed atmosphere. Six luxurious double bedrooms are available, each with its own fantasy bathroom with spa bath and shower. Every facility is offered including colour television, direct dial telephone, radio and tea making facilities. Four poster rooms. Ideal honeymoon setting. Heated swimming pool. Superb riding country, stabling available for own horse. Close to excellent yachting resorts and several good golf courses. Christmas house party. *ETB* 👑 👑 👑 👑.

Herefordshire

THE STEPPES COUNTRY HOUSE HOTEL,
Ullingswick, Near Hereford,
Herefordshire HR1 3JG

Tel: 0432 820424

Residential licence; 3 bedrooms, all with private bathrooms; Historic interest; Children over 12 and dogs welcome; Car park (6); Hereford 8 miles.

Sometimes the traveller has to wander off the beaten track to find something truly original and the Steppes, peacefully resting in the tiny Wye Valley hamlet of Ullingswick, will more than repay those who visit it. This charming, creeper-clad country hotel is furnished and decorated entirely in keeping with its seventeenth century character, whilst modern comforts have been expertly incorporated into the individually styled bedrooms, complete with television, clock/radio and tea/coffee-making facilities. The Cordon Bleu cuisine is under the personal supervision of Mrs. Tricia Howland, for whom each dinner served is a special occasion, appealing particularly to those with more adventurous tastes, and deserving of the best locally-grown vegetables, home-baked bread, and eggs from the hotel's own hens. And what better, after an ample breakfast, than to tour the area's ancient villages, walk in the Black Mountains and Malvern Hills, visit the porcelain works, a local cider mill or the famous cattle market. Prices, including dinner, breakfast, and en suite facilities from £28 per night.

Taking a pet on holiday? Then buy
"PETS WELCOME!"

THE ANIMAL LOVERS' HOLIDAY GUIDE
Details of Hotels, Guest Houses, Furnished Accommodation, Caravans, etc. where holiday makers and their pets are made welcome.
*Available from most newsagents and bookshops price £1.95
or from Publishers (please add 30p postage)*
**FHG PUBLICATIONS LTD
Abbey Mill Business Centre, Seedhill,
Paisley, Renfrewshire PA1 1JN**

WYE RAPIDS HOTEL,
Symonds Yat West, Ross-on-Wye,
Herefordshire

Tel: 0600 890366

Residential and restaurant licence; 15 bedrooms, all with baths or showers; Children and dogs welcome; Car park (20); Gloucester 20 miles, Hereford 17, Ross-on-Wye 6, Monmouth 5.

Among the famous beauty spots of England there are few to compare with and none to surpass Symonds Yat Gorge in the heart of the Wye Valley. At the most dramatically beautiful spot in the gorge — an area of 'Outstanding Natural Beauty' — stands this charming country house hotel in five acres of terraced gardens overlooking the wooded slopes to the Yat Rock and the Wye Rapids. There is much to see and do in this unspoilt haven for lovers of the countryside. There is a residents' TV lounge, bridge room and cocktail bar. A particularly attractive feature is the spacious terrace on which to relax and fully appreciate the magnificent scenery. Both table d'hôte and à la carte meals are available in the tastefully decorated diningroom and lunches may be taken in the vine-covered sun lounge. The emphasis is on quiet relaxation. *AA**, RAC**; Ashley Courtenay recommended; ETB* ♨ ♨ ♨.

THE CROFT COUNTRY GUEST HOUSE,
Vowchurch, Hereford,
Herefordshire HR2 0QE

Tel: 0981 6226

From early 1989: 0981 550-226

Residential licence; 7 bedrooms, all with private bathrooms; Car park (10); London 135 miles, Gloucester 35, Worcester 30, Hereford 10, Pontrilas 6.

The Croft is a charming and intimate country house where guests may be assured of the best of personal attention from resident owners Amy and Graham Spencer. Standing in 6½ acres of mature and secluded gardens and paddocks and commanding glorious views over the lovely Golden Valley to the mountains beyond, this is an ideal base for exploring the beautiful and unspoilt region of the Marches and border country. Individually-furnished bedrooms are well-appointed and all enjoy superb views. Traditional and imaginative British cooking is a feature on the menu, as are favourite Continental dishes, and much of the fruit and vegetables on the menu come from The Croft's own gardens. *BTA Country Guest House Commendation Award; RAC Highly Acclaimed. AA Selected. ETB* ♨ ♨ ♨.

HOPE END HOTEL,
Hope End, Ledbury,
Herefordshire HR8 1JQ

Tel: 0531 3613*

Restaurant and residential licence; 9 bedrooms, all with private bathrooms; Historic interest; Car park (10); Gloucester 17 miles.

Brightly furnished and set amidst 40 acres of wooded parkland near the Malvern Hills, Hope End is the home of John and Patricia Hegarty. It follows that one of the salient attractions here is the food, for Patricia Hegarty is famous as the creator of memorable recipes in the English country tradition, her superb dishes being supported by an outstanding selection of wines. The house is historically interesting and was once the home of Elizabeth Barrett Browning. Now renovated in lavish style and with many antiques on view, this delightful little hotel is the epitome of comfort and the ideal setting for a peaceful holiday with many lovely walks in the vicinity.

THE ARCHES,
Walford Road, Ross-on-Wye,
Herefordshire HR9 5DT

Tel: 0989 63348*

Restaurant and residential licence; 8 bedrooms, 2 with private bathrooms; Children welcome; dogs by arrangement; Car park (8); Gloucester 17 miles.

The Arches is a small family-run hotel set in half an acre of lawns, ideally situated only a few minutes' walk from the town centre. All bedrooms are furnished to a high standard and have views of the lawned garden. Tea making facilities are available in bedrooms, also optional colour television. Attractive residents' lounge with colour television. Excellent home cooking, using fresh produce whenever possible. Ample parking. Central heating. A warm and friendly atmosphere with personal service. Children at reduced rates, based on sharing. *Les Routiers, AA Listed, RAC Acclaimed, ETB* 🌑 🌑.

GLEWSTONE COURT,
Near Ross-on-Wye,
Herefordshire HR9 6AW

Tel: 098984 367

Licensed; 7 bedrooms, all with private bathrooms; Historic interest; Children and pets welcome; Car park (20); Gloucester 17 miles.

The Hotel is a spacious and elegant listed country house offering its guests the most convivial and friendly welcome, set in its own grounds of some three acres and surrounded by fruit orchards. All the pretty bedrooms are large and comfortable with their own bathrooms and lead onto the galleried porticoed landing that is an outstanding feature of the house. Food is always freshly prepared to the highest standards using local seasonal ingredients under the personal supervision of Christine Reeve-Tucker whilst William looks after the Drawing Room Bar with its open log fire and deep comfortable settees. Hot air ballooning is a speciality of the hotel. *ETB* 🌑 🌑 🌑

NOTE

All the information in this book is given in good faith in the belief that it is correct. However, the publishers cannot guarantee the facts given in these pages, neither are they responsible for changes in policy, ownership or terms that may take place after the date of going to press. Readers should always satisfy themselves that the facilities they require are available and that the terms, if quoted, still apply.

WOODLEA HOTEL,
Symonds Yat West, Ross-on-Wye, Herefordshire HR9 6BL

Tel: 0600 890206*

Restaurant and residential licence; 9 bedrooms, 5 with private bathrooms; Children and dogs welcome; Car park (9); Ross-on-Wye 5 miles, Monmouth 4.

This family run licensed Victorian hotel is set in a secluded woodland valley overlooking the famous Wye Rapids. It is an ideal holiday and touring centre just a mile from the A40, between nearby Monmouth and Ross-on-Wye, with numerous local attractions. Double, twin, single and family rooms are available, most en-suite, all equipped to a modern standard, and fully centrally heated. There is a colour TV lounge, reading lounge, separate well stocked bar and wine list, and a spacious dining room which serves an imaginative and distinctive menu. The hotel has its own outdoor swimming pool.

PENCRAIG COURT HOTEL AND RESTAURANT,
Pencraig, Near Ross-on-Wye, Herefordshire HR9 6HR

Tel: 098-984 306*

Residential and restaurant licence; 11 bedrooms, all with private bathrooms; Historic interest; Children welcome; Car park (25); Ross-on-Wye 4 miles.

Standing high above the banks of the River Wye, Pencraig Court Hotel proudly surveys the beautiful countryside of this serene part of rural England. Constructed nearly 200 years ago, the hotel retains the elegance and furnishings of the Georgian era but has been sympatheti-cally updated so that all bedrooms now have private bath, colour television and tea/coffee making facilities. One such room also has a four-poster bed. Duncan and Celia Sykes have run the hotel since 1973. In the hotel restaurant guests can enjoy the very best in English and French cuisine and sample a fine selection of inexpensive and interesting wines from our cellar. Prices from £29.50 for dinner, bed and English breakfast. Free colour brochure on request.

Hertfordshire

REDCOATS FARMHOUSE HOTEL,
Redcoats Green, Near Hitchin,
Hertfordshire SG4 7JR
Tel: 0438 729500*

Licensed; 14 bedrooms, 12 with private bathrooms; Historic interest; Children welcome, dogs by arrangement; Car park (60); Bedford 17 miles, Luton 9.

It was only a few minutes from the busy A1 that the peace of the soft, undulating Hertfordshire countryside exerted its influence, inducing a feeling of pleasurable anticipation and relaxation, a mood substantiated by acquaintance with this lovely 15th century farmhouse hotel. Within its mellow walls, all is old English charm with beams and fine antique furniture promoting an easy-going atmosphere. Recommended is a visit to the bar before sampling the excellent traditional English and Continental cuisine which features local fish, game and vegetables. Guest rooms, most with bath or shower, are comfortably furnished and have great character whilst there are good facilities for small conferences and parties. Ask for details of bargain-break weekends.

BRIGGENS HOUSE HOTEL,
Stanstead Abbots, Ware,
Hertfordshire SG12 8LD
Tel: 027-979 2416

Licensed; 54 bedrooms, all with private bathrooms; Historic interest; Children welcome; Car park (70); Cambridge 30 miles.

The wish to escape into a world of elegance and tranquillity need not involve an arduous journey for it can be found in this most elegant eighteenth century Stately Home. Set in 45 acres of softly rolling Hertfordshire countryside, Briggens House is an oasis of good living in the true traditions of yesteryear. As befits the high standards set by the Norfolk Capital Group of Hotels, public and guest rooms have been meticulously and tastefully restored and are lavish in their luxurious appointments. The kitchens are under the expert supervision of Master Chef Richard Duckworth, the cuisine being both beautifully presented and imaginative. A peaceful retreat this may be, but there are the opportunities for such active pursuits as Golf, Tennis, Swimming, Croquet, Boules, Fishing and, for that special treat, Clay Pigeon Shooting.

---

* The appearance of an asterisk after the telephone number indicates that the hotel in question is closed for a period during the winter months. Exact dates should be ascertained from the hotel itself.

Isle of Man

THE GRAND ISLAND HOTEL,
Ramsey,
Isle of Man

Tel: 0624 812455

Licensed; 55 bedrooms, 49 with private facilities; Children welcome; Car park (150); Point of Ayre 7 miles.

The Grand Island Hotel is the Isle of Man's most prestigious hotel. It offers 55 luxury bedrooms including 7 elegant suites. Also available is a health and leisure spa with wave swimming pool. Superb food with international cuisine is served in the Bay Room restaurant and continental specialities are available in the Vollan Bistro. All only five minutes away from Ramsey Golf Course. Special green fees exclusive to the hotel. *AA, RAC****, IOMTB 5 Keys.*

Other specialised

FHG PUBLICATIONS

* Recommended SHORT-BREAK HOLIDAYS IN BRITAIN   £2.95

* Recommended WAYSIDE INNS OF BRITAIN   £2.95

* PETS WELCOME!   £1.95

* BED AND BREAKFAST IN BRITAIN   £1.95

Published annually. Please add 30p postage (U.K. only) when ordering from the publishers:

FHG PUBLICATIONS LTD
Abbey Mill Business Centre, Seedhill,
Paisley, Renfrewshire PA1 1JN

Isle of Wight

ALVERSTON MANOR HOTEL,
Luccombe Road, Shanklin,
Isle of Wight PO37 6RR

Tel: 0983 862586

Residential licence; 12 bedrooms, 10 with private bathrooms; Children welcome; Car park (15); Newport 10 miles, Sandown 2.

A warm welcome is assured at Alverston Manor, an elegant Victorian Country House built a little over a century ago. Situated in one of the most beautiful parts of Shanklin, there are magnificent views over Sandown Bay and the surrounding countryside. Within the hotel there is a main lounge with colour TV and an extensive balcony with superb sea views. The bedrooms are fully heated and comfortably furnished. Large landscaped garden including heated swimming pool, putting green and grass tennis court.

Please mention
Recommended COUNTRY HOTELS
when seeking refreshment or
accommodation at a Hotel
mentioned in these pages

BOURNE HALL COUNTRY HOTEL,
Shanklin,
Isle of Wight PO37 6RR

Tel: 0983 862820*

Residential and restaurant licence; 28 bedrooms, 3 family suites, honeymoon suites, all with private bathrooms; Children welcome; Car park (20); London 81 miles, Cowes 15, Newport 10.

Informality and a friendly welcome are the hallmarks of Bourne Hall, a pleasant country hotel standing in its own three acre grounds at the foot of the Luccombe Downs and close to the sea and the Old Village. However, if exploring is not to your taste there are plenty of activities on site, including tennis, badminton, croquet, sauna, solarium, jacuzzi and indoor and outdoor pools. And for those who have worked up an appetite, the hotel offers ample and delicious meals and snacks. Children are welcome and can be accommodated in family rooms, whilst the more romantic might like to try one of the honeymoon suites. *ETB* 🌷 🌷 🌷 🌷.

THE NODES COUNTRY HOTEL,
Alum Bay, Old Road, Totland Bay,
Isle of Wight

Tel: 0983 752859*

Residential and restaurant licence; 11 bedrooms, 8 with private bathrooms; Children and pets welcome; Car park (15); Newport 12 miles, Yarmouth 4.

Full of atmosphere, this charming Victorian country house nestles at the foot of Tennyson Downs in its own two and a half acres of grounds. Superb walks may be enjoyed in the glorious West Wight countryside and there are many safe, sandy beaches nearby. Concentrating on traditional country cooking, the cuisine is excellent and drinks are served in the convivial Courtyard Bar where hot beverages are also available in the evening. A well-stocked wine cellar complements the appetising dishes. There is a golf practice net within the grounds of the hotel and there are also facilities for table tennis, darts and badminton. For lovers of rural tranquillity allied to good service, this is a perfect spot for a holiday.

Kent

HOWFIELD MANOR,
Chartham Hatch, Canterbury,
Kent CT4 7HQ

Tel: 0227 738294

Restaurant and residential licence; 13 bedrooms, all with private bathrooms; Historic interest; Children over 10 welcome; Car park (46); London 62 miles, Maidstone 25, Canterbury 2.

In the heart of the lovely Kent countryside and convenient for the myriad attractions of Canterbury and several seaside resorts, this comfortable, family-run hotel is a recommended holiday base. Homely and tranquil, the hotel has accommodation of a high order and it is an easy place in which to relax and reassess life. The restaurant is open for lunch and dinner, and serves a set menu as well as an à la carte. We also offer a function room for larger parties. Central heating is installed throughout and log fires burn in the inglenook fireplaces in the sittingroom and library/television room on winter evenings.

PLEASE ENCLOSE A STAMPED
ADDRESSED ENVELOPE WHEN
WRITING TO ENQUIRE ABOUT
ACCOMMODATION FEATURED IN
THIS GUIDE

WOODPECKERS COUNTRY HOTEL,
Womenswold, Near Canterbury,
Kent
Tel: 022-782 319

Residential and restaurant licence; 15 bedrooms, 6 with private bathrooms; Dover 9 miles, Canterbury 7.

A really first-rate country holiday venue for families, this former rectory presents the most helpful amenities for parents and their charges. Throughout, there is a friendly and informal atmosphere to which the young, in particular, will instantly respond. Bedrooms include a four-poster, brass bedstead, Georgian and bridal bedrooms, all en suite and with colour television and tea and coffee making facilities. There are two comfortable lounges, one with television and a selection of children's games, and a luxury bar. The grounds extend to two acres and incorporate a heated swimming pool, swing, slide, sandpit and pets corner. Extremely popular with guests of all ages is the excellent traditional English cuisine served by a willing staff under the kindly supervision of proprietors Pat and Ted Millard.

TUDOR ARMS HOTEL,
Hawkhurst,
Kent
Tel: 058-05 2312

Licensed; 20 bedrooms, most with private bathrooms; Historic interest; Children welcome; Car park (40), garages (2); Maidstone 17 miles, Rye 13, Hurst Green 3.

A charming hotel with a country pub atmosphere, the Tudor Arms is a warm and friendly, well-run establishment with a restaurant that is open to non-residents. Here is the setting for imaginative and well-planned dishes, all skilfully prepared by an experienced chef who enjoys cooking with locally grown produce. The hotel's extensive grounds, which include a children's play area, are well kept and have shaded lawns and colourful flower beds. The lovely Weald of Kent invites closer acquaintace on all sides and jaunts to the coast may be made by way of variety. Bedrooms are well appointed, all having private bathrooms and colour television. There are two bars as well as a sunny lounge. A colour brochure and tariff available on request from resident manager Mr David Hill. *AA**, RAC**; ETB* 👑 👑 👑.

Lancashire

THE PICKERINGS,
Garstang Road, Catterall,
Lancashire PR3 0HA

Tel: 09-952 2100/2133

Restaurant licence; 9 bedrooms, all with private bathrooms; Car park; Blackpool 12 miles, Lancaster 10.

The Pickerings is a delightful country house set in acres of floodlit gardens. The tasteful and elegant surroundings complement the flair and ability of the team of chefs. Head Chef Nigel Marsden is a master in the art of cooking whilst proprietor Allan Leck is on hand to ensure the high standards are constantly maintained. Dinner is a five course affair, lunch a more modest three. Specialities can include Avocado Fool with Tipsy Shrimps, Sirloin Steak stuffed with Crab, or Lymeswold Fritters with Cumberland Sauce. Vegetarians may choose the Stilton, Celery and Walnut Pie, or the Vegetable Vindaloo. Fine wines include an excellent House Champagne. Upstairs are delightful en suite bedrooms and bridal suites — each individually furnished (three with four-poster beds and two with whirlpool baths). Other comforts include colour television, tea/coffee making facilities and hairdryers.

THE SPREAD EAGLE HOTEL,
Sawley, Near Clitheroe,
Lancashire BB7 4NH

Tel: 0200 41202/41406

Licensed; 10 bedrooms, all with private facilities; Historic interest; Children welcome; Car park (80); Skipton 19 miles, Preston 18.

The Spread Eagle Hotel lies on a picturesque bend of the River Ribble and the large picture windows afford wonderful views of the river and surrounding countryside. Its situation and good food have made it a popular meeting place for years. The bars offer a wide choice of drinks including the well known Theakstons Bitter and the locally popular Thwaites on draught. Renowned for its excellent cuisine and service the hotel is open for luncheons and dinners every day. Each of the 10 bedrooms has private bathroom or shower room, colour television, radio alarm, telephone, heating, tea-coffee making facilities. Many walks and places of historical interest nearby.

LANE HEAD,
Millhouses, Wray, Lancaster,
Lancashire LA2 8NF

Tel: 05242 21148

Restaurant licence; 4 bedrooms, all with private bathrooms or shower rooms; Historic interest; Car park; Kirkby Lonsdale 7 miles.

Situated in the heart of the Lune Valley, parts of Lane Head date back to the 1700's but the old farmhouse has been tastefully renovated and extended to combine old world charm with high quality accommodation. You will enjoy the peaceful hill views from the bedrooms while the diningroom overlooks the garden, stream and pond. Home cooking with fresh produce is a speciality. The Lake District, Yorkshire Dales and even the coast are within easy reach. Historic houses, halls and castles, villages and old churches are just a short drive away. Lane Head is a comfortable and relaxing base to explore this area of unspoilt natural beauty. *ETB* 🌷 🌷 🌷.

TREE TOPS MOTEL AND RESTAURANT,
Southport Old Road, Formby,
Merseyside

Tel: 07-048 79651

Licensed; 11 bedrooms, some with private bathrooms; Car park; Liverpool 13 miles, Southport 8.

Tree Tops is renowned for the outstanding quality of French and English cuisine. Exquisitely furnished and all accommodation has colour television, radio, telephone and tea/coffee making facilities. Heated swimming pool available May to September. Set in five acres of beautiful wooded grounds with no parking problems. Only minutes from five championship golf courses. *Ashley Courtenay Recommended, ETB* 🌷 🌷 🌷 🌷.

Leicestershire

SYSONBY KNOLL HOTEL,
Asfordby Road, Melton Mowbray,
Leicestershire LE13 0HP

Tel: 0664 63563*

Residential and restaurant licence; 25 bedrooms, 19 with private bathrooms; Children and dogs welcome; Car park (30); Nottingham 20 miles, Leicester 15.

An excursion into the hunting heart of England will be assured of success judging by the warm welcome extended by the principals of this fine hotel. With two acres of grounds bordered by the tinkling River Eye, the hotel is just a mile from the town centre and possesses amenities that measure up to purposely exacting requirements — a most satisfying place in which to stay, facilities including well-furnished bedrooms (one with four-poster), mostly with bathrooms en suite, delightful lounge, bar and private conference and dining rooms, whilst the table d'hôte and extensive à la carte cuisine is first-rate. There is a swimming pool in the grounds and a pitch and putt course and riding stable nearby.

Taking a pet on holiday? Then buy
"PETS WELCOME!"

THE ANIMAL LOVERS' HOLIDAY GUIDE
Details of Hotels, Guest Houses, Furnished Accommodation, Caravans, etc. where
holiday makers and their pets are made welcome.
Available from most newsagents and bookshops price £1.95
or from Publishers (please add 30p postage)
FHG PUBLICATIONS LTD
Abbey Mill Business Centre, Seedhill,
Paisley, Renfrewshire PA1 1JN

Lincolnshire

BOURNE EAU HOUSE,
South Street, Bourne,
Lincolnshire PE10 9LY

Tel: 0778 423621

Unlicensed; 3 bedrooms, all with private bathrooms; Historic interest; Children and dogs by arrangement; Car park (4); Lincoln 30 miles, Spalding 10, Stamford 10.

Oak beams and inglenooks give a clue to the Elizabethan origins of this mellow and charming house and various Jacobean and Georgian features were later added. As attractive and as historically interesting as the accommodation facilities is the position of the house. A stream borders the extensive gardens; just beyond, lies Bourne's twelfth century abbey and opposite this listed house is the site of Hereward the Wake's castle and the home of his mother, Lady Godiva. There is central heating, and log fires exude warmth in the traditional manner in the Jacobean dining and music rooms. Other magnificent reception rooms include a drawing room and library.

GARDEN HOUSE HOTEL,
St. Martin's, Stamford,
Lincolnshire PE9 2LP

Tel: 0780 63359 Telex: 329230

Licensed; 21 bedrooms, all with private bathrooms; Historic interest; Children and dogs welcome; Car park (30); Melton Mowbray 21 miles.

In keeping with the fine stone town of Stamford and nearby Burghley House, this mellow building has changed little over the years. It dates back to 1796 but was only transformed into a first-class hotel by the present Hosts, Richard and Janet Gorrie, in 1982. Incorporating an adjoining house and tastefully modernised, the hotel impresses with its contemporary facilities although the grace of ages still casts its spell. Guest rooms are equipped with colour television, radio and direct-dial telephone and some of family size are available. Good wholesome cooking is a feature of the fare served in a dining room hung with attractive tapestries. The St. Martin's Room is specially equipped for conferences and functions.

WASHINGBOROUGH HALL COUNTRY HOUSE HOTEL,
Church Hill, Washingborough, Lincoln,
Lincolnshire LN4 1BE
Tel: 0522 790340

Licensed; 12 bedrooms, all with private bathroom; Historic interest; Children and dogs welcome; Car park (50); Horncastle 17 miles, Lincoln 4.

Impressive Lincoln and its splendid hilltop cathedral may be the motivating reason for acquainting oneself with Washingborough Hall which is only 2½ miles away. As solidly British as the square tower of the adjacent village church, this delightful country house hotel is also ideally placed for quiet holidays with the Lincolnshire Wolds, Nottinghamshire and even the east coast within easy reach. Beautfully furnished public rooms and bedrooms with en suite facilities, colour television, radio and direct-dial telephone await discerning guests and the à la carte cuisine is varied and imaginative. The house stands in three acres of lawns and woodland where one may swim in the pool or play croquet. Opportunities for fishing, golf, riding and squash exist close by.

HELP IMPROVE BRITISH TOURIST STANDARDS

You are choosing holiday accommodation from our very popular FHG Publications. Whether it be a hotel, guest house, farmhouse or self-catering accommodation, we think you will find it hospitable, comfortable and clean, and your host and hostess friendly and helpful. Why not write and tell us about it?

As a recognition of the generally well-run and excellent holiday accommodation reviewed in our publications, we at FHG Publications Ltd. present a diploma to proprietors who receive the highest recommendation from their guests who are also readers of our Guides. If you care to write to us praising the holiday you have booked through FHG Publications Ltd. – whether this be board, self-catering accommodation, a sporting or a caravan holiday, what you say will be evaluated and the proprietors who reach our final list will be contacted.

The winning proprietor will receive an attractive framed diploma to display on his premises as recognition of a high standard of comfort, amenity and hospitality. FHG Publications Ltd. offer this diploma as a contribution towards the improvement of standards in tourist accommodation in Britain. Help your excellent host or hostess to win it!

FHG DIPLOMA

We nominate ....

....

Because

Name ....

Address ....

.... Telephone No. ....

West Midlands

NEW HALL,
Walmley Road, Sutton Coldfield,
West Midlands B76 8QX

Tel: 021 378 2442

Licensed; 65 bedrooms, all with private bathrooms; Historic interest; Well-behaved children welcome; Dogs by arrangement; Car park (80); Oxford 68, Warwick 39, Stratford-upon-Avon 34 miles.

Reputed to be the oldest moated manor house in England — parts of the original house date back to the 12th century — New Hall is now a luxury country house hotel and restaurant. Run by Ian and Caroline Parkes, their style, imagination and attention to detail ensure that the welcome which guests receive reflects the finest aspects and past traditions of a grand family home. The bedrooms are beautifully furnished. New Hall's chef, Allan Garth, has consistently won recognition as one of the most talented chefs in the country — with rosettes from both the AA and Michelin — and his food, unmistakably English, is set off perfectly by the attractive oak-panelled restaurant. Special weekend and short break rates are available.

RECOMMENDED SHORT-BREAK HOLIDAYS
IN BRITAIN

Introduced by John Carter, TV Holiday Expert and Journalist

Specifically designed to cater for the most rapidly growing sector of the holiday market in the UK. Illustrated details of hotels offering special 'Bargain Breaks' throughout the year.

Available from newsagents and bookshops or direct from the publishers:
£2.95 plus 30p postage.

FHG PUBLICATIONS LTD
Abbey Mill Business Centre, Seedhill,
Paisley, Renfrewshire PA1 1JN

Norfolk

SHERBOURNE COUNTRY HOUSE HOTEL,
Norwich Road, Attleborough,
Norfolk NR17 2JX

Tel: 0953 454363

Licensed; 9 bedrooms, 7 with private bathrooms; Historic interest; Car park (50); London 100 miles, Norwich 14, Diss 12.

A small part-sixteenth-century country house in mature grounds enjoying an open outlook over the countryside of south Norfolk. With Sherbourne's notable distinction of a mention in an eighteenth-century survey of the buildings of England, the aim of the proprietors is to build on and maintain that welcoming old world atmosphere of a friendly country house, with open fires and period furnishings. All bedrooms are individually furnished in period style, some with four-poster beds, all with direct dial telephone, colour television and tea/coffee making facilities. International and traditional English cuisine is offered in the elegant diningroom or comfortable bar. *ETB* 🌷🌷🌷, *AA***.

BUNWELL MANOR HOTEL,
Bunwell, Near Norwich,
Norfolk

Tel: 095-389 8304*

Licensed; 10 bedrooms, all with private shower/bathrooms; Historic interest; Children welcome; Car park (30); Norwich 12 miles, Diss 9.

Although tastefully modernised, there is ample evidence of the sixteenth-century origins of this graceful house which combines charm and character with the distinctive service expected by the guest of today. Beneath the beamed ceilings, all rooms are centrally heated, attractively furnished and have their own facilities. The hotel has a warm country feel about it and Mr and Mrs Nylk (the proprietors) take a personal interest in the welfare of their guests and the à la carte menu is varied and interesting. The Tudor diningroom is very distinctive and the Regency bar overlooks the garden and the lawns. The hotel stands in its own grounds on the edge of a very peaceful village, but central to all the Norfolk holiday activities. *ETB* 🌷🌷🌷, *AA**, RAC***.

CROWN HOTEL,
Bridge Street, Downham Market, Norfolk

Tel: 0366 382322

Licensed; 10 bedrooms, 7 with private bathrooms; Historic interest; Car park (50); London 88 miles, Ely 17, Swaffham 15, King's Lynn 11.

This lovely old seventeenth century coaching inn has a fine Jacobean staircase leading to modern and well-appointed bedrooms. There is a charming old-world bar and beamed diningroom, the latter the setting for really excellent meals with practically everything home-made from the soup and pâté to the gateaux on the sweet trolley. Vegetables are always fresh and there is an ample wine list. Prices are reasonable indeed and credit is due to Owners Sue and John Champion, who present such fine English cooking and helpful service. Rooms are available for private dinner parties and the Stables Grill and cold table is open seven days a week. Good beers and snacks complement the traditional appeal of this quiet retreat which is also a fine touring centre. Weekend breaks may be arranged.

LENWADE HOUSE HOTEL,
Great Witchingham, Norwich, Norfolk NR9 5QP

Tel: 0603 872288

Licensed; 14 bedrooms, all with private bathrooms; Children over 5 and dogs welcome; Car park; Great Yarmouth 20 miles.

The 18 acres of beautiful woods and lawns which surround this charming country house incorporate many attractions for the sporting holidaymaker. There are three grass tennis courts, two squash courts, croquet lawn, putting green, heated outdoor pool and a lake well stocked with rainbow and brown trout. Horse riding holidays may also be arranged. Accommodation and service maintain the high reputation of this impressive hotel. All guest rooms have private bath facilities, colour television and several other thoughtful appointments.

GREEN FARM HOTEL & RESTAURANT,
Thorpe Market, Norwich, Norfolk NR11 8TH

Tel: 026-379 602*

Restaurant and residential licence; 6 bedrooms; Historic interest; Children and pets welcome; Car park (70); Great Yarmouth 20 miles.

Green Farm is situated in the delightful Norfolk village of Thorpe Market, within easy reach of the beautiful Norfolk coast, the famous Norfolk Broads and the historical city of Norwich. The house dates back to the 16th century. The beautiful flint exterior and original door frames give the house a character all of its own. Each of the five bedrooms has been modernised whilst preserving its individual character. All rooms have antique beds, colour television, tea and coffee making facilities and en suite bathrooms. In the restaurant the chef proprietor uses fresh, local produce. *ETB* 🌷 🌷 🌷.

POUND GREEN HOTEL,
Shipdham, Dereham,
Norfolk 1P25 7LS
Tel: 0362 820165

Licensed; 15 bedrooms, 7 with private bathrooms; Children and pets welcome; Car park (70); London 106 miles, Norwich 20, Dereham 5.

Set in the lovely Norfolk countryside in one acre of its own attractive and secluded gardens stands this AA recommended hotel. Proprietors Mr and Mrs Johnson pride themselves on the quality of Pound Green's cuisine, with a wide choice available including set and full à la carte menus and featuring vegetarian dishes. And after a meal, guests can take advantage of the leisure activities available, including a pool table and heated outdoor swimming pool, while nearby are many of the attractions of this lovely corner of England: golf and sporting facilities, country footpaths and forests, historic houses and the coast. *ETB* 🌸 🌸 🌸.

SHIPDHAM PLACE,
Shipdham, Near Thetford,
Norfolk 1P25 7LX
Tel: 0362 820303

Restaurant and residential licence; 8 bedrooms, all with private bathrooms; Historic interest; Children and dogs welcome; Car park (25); Norwich 20 miles.

A lovely 17th century rectory with attractive later additions, Shipdham Place is described as a restaurant with rooms and, therefore, cuisine is the first consideration and rightly so, for through the expertise of Resident Directors Alan and Tina Poulton the imaginative dishes and wines are acquiring a wide reputation for their excellence. A set 5-course dinner is served and each day a special salad is prepared; there is also an appetising selection of farmhouse and French cheeses. At lunchtime, a simple selection of light lunches will be available to residents. The accommodation is homely, each room having its own bathroom, featuring marble-topped basins, cast-iron baths and WC's with solid wooden seats, the acme of Victorian comfort.

ELDERTON LODGE HOTEL,
Thorpe Market, North Walsham,
Norfolk NR11 8TZ
Tel: 026-379 547

Licensed; 8 bedrooms, 2 with private bathrooms; Historic interest; Children and dogs welcome; Car park (30); Cromer 4 miles.

Situated on the edge of the Gunton Park estate, this comfortable and well-appointed house was once the Dower House and dates mainly from the Georgian period. The setting is beautiful and peaceful with red and fallow deer roaming the park and there is a large lake available for fishing. Conveniently placed for excursions to the Broads and coast, the hotel offers attractive accommodation. Full central heating is installed and guest rooms are handsomely equipped. Backed by willing service, the cuisine is of a high order, the table d'hôte menu presenting an appetising and wide choice of imaginative dishes at most reasonable prices.

Northumberland

BISHOPFIELD COUNTRY HOUSE HOTEL,
Allendale, Hexham,
Northumberland NE47 9EJ

Tel: 043-483 248

Residential licence; 11 bedrooms, all with en suite facilities, telephone and colour TV; Historic interest; Children welcome, dogs in car; Car park (20); Haydon Bridge 5 miles.

A fine eighteenth century country house hotel standing in 50 acres of beautiful countryside and offering peace, tranquillity and relaxation in charming surroundings. Proprietors Keith and Kathy Fairless's insistence on the very highest standards of accommodation and cuisine has earned Bishopfield an excellent reputation for its home cooked meals, ranging from snacks to full dinners, and served in the attractive dining room. All bedrooms have full central heating, private facilities and colour television. Edwardian snooker room with full size table is a recent addition. Private trout fishing available, also bicycles and pick-up service for walkers.

BREAMISH HOUSE HOTEL,
Powburn, Alnwick,
Northumberland NE66 4LL

Tel: 066-578 266*

Restaurant and residential licence; 10 bedrooms, all with private bathrooms; Historic interest; Children over 12 years welcome; Car park (30); Berwick-upon-Tweed 30 miles.

Gloriously placed for excursions into an area abounding in natural beauty, the gracious, Georgian-style Breamish House stands in 5 acres of woodland and gardens beneath the Cheviot Hills and adjacent to the lovely Coquet Valley. To the east lies the romantic and sandy Northumbrian coast and all around are unspoilt villages and places of historic interest. A farmhouse in the 17th century and now refurbished to exacting modern standards, this comfortable and tranquil haven takes pride in its Cordon Bleu cuisine and caring service. An elegant drawing room allows relaxation in the evening before retiring to comfortable bedrooms, all equipped with colour television, radio, telephone, tea and coffee making facilities.

RIVERDALE HALL HOTEL AND RESTAURANT,
Bellingham, Hexham,
Northumberland

Tel: 0660 20254

Licensed; 20 bedrooms, all with private bathrooms; Children and dogs welcome; Car park (60); Hexham 17 miles, Kielder Water 8.

Set in Northumberland National Park, this is the nearest hotel to Kielder Water and Forest. Popular with the sporting enthusiast, Riverdale Hall has its own indoor swimming pool, games room, sauna, cricket field and salmon and trout river and just opposite is Bellingham's golf course. The Pennine Way and National Trust walks pass through the town, and Hadrian's Wall is nearby. The hotel is centrally heated throughout, and much character is added by log fires and four-poster beds. The restaurant is renowned for a high standard of cuisine. John Cocker, resident owner, is a keen sportsman and a friendly host. *ETB* 🌼 🌼 🌼 🌼.

TILLMOUTH PARK HOTEL,
Cornhill-on-Tweed,
Northumberland TD12 4UU

Tel: 0890 2255

Licensed; 13 bedrooms, all with private bathrooms; Historic interest; Children and dogs welcome; Car park (70); London 333 miles, Newcastle-on-Tyne 59, Alnwick 30, Berwick-upon-Tweed 13, Kelso 10, Coldstream 2.

On the very doorstep of Scotland, amongst the rolling countryside of North Northumberland lies this imposing Victorian mansion. It is ideally situated for visiting many places of interest on either side of the border, while guests who enjoy fishing will rush to take advantage of the hotel's five miles of water on the River Tweed. All the bedrooms have private bathrooms and these include the Sir Walter Scott Room with its twin four poster beds. Before sampling the excellent cuisine, one may partake of an aperitif by a log fire in the bar and, having dined, relax in the galleried lounge with its massive stone fireplace.

PLEASE ENCLOSE A STAMPED

ADDRESSED ENVELOPE WHEN

WRITING TO ENQUIRE ABOUT

ACCOMMODATION FEATURED IN

THIS GUIDE

LINDEN HALL HOTEL,
Longhorsley, Morpeth,
Northumberland NE65 8XG

Tel: 0670 516611 Telex: 538224
Fax: 0670 88544

Licensed; 45 bedrooms plus two cottages, all with private bathrooms; Historic interest; Children and dogs welcome; Car park (260); Coldstream 38 miles, Morpeth 7.

Linden Park is a magnificent Georgian House, situated in 300 acres of splendid park and woodland in mid Northumberland. Visitors to Linden Hall can be assured of a warm welcome, together with elegant surroundings, and a tradition of personal service that gives the hotel a unique and friendly atmosphere. Each bedroom is individually decorated and furnished, fully equipped with hairdryer, radio, colour television, direct dial telephone and baby listening service. The Dobson Restaurant offers you a delightful menu in graceful surroundings with panoramic views east over the croquet lawn to the rugged Northumberland coastline and south over formal gardens to parkland beyond. The Monck Cocktail Bar is a soothing venue for a pre-dinner drink or to meet friends. *AA, RAC****; ETB* 🌺 🌺 🌺 🌺 🌺.

OTTERBURN TOWER HOTEL,
Otterburn,
Northumberland

Tel: 0830 20620

Licensed; 12 bedrooms, 5 with private bathrooms; Historic interest; Children and dogs welcome; Car park (50); Newcastle 32 miles.

This imposing fortress-like mansion was created in Victorian times around an original structure built in 1076 by a cousin of William the Conqueror. Set on the edge of the Northumberland National Park in its own grounds, the Tower is steeped in history and even has its own ghost, that of Mad Jack Hall who was executed in 1716 for high treason. Peace reigns today, however, and guests may look forward to good English food and service and excellent accommodation, some rooms having four-poster beds. The hotel holds fishing rights on a wide stretch of the River Rede and, as a base for touring Northumbria and the Border Country, is heartily recommended.

WHITTON FARM HOTEL,
Rothbury,
Northumberland NE65 7RL

Tel: 0669 20811*

Licensed; 20 bedrooms, 10 with private bathrooms; Historic interest; Children and dogs welcome; Car park (30); Newcastle upon Tyne 30 miles, Alnwick 12.

With exposed beams and original stonework blending in subtle fashion with up-to-date appointments and charming furnishings, this early Victorian house in the Coquet Valley exhibits great character as well as most appetising home-made food. In keeping with its former function as a farmhouse, the atmosphere is warm and informal and from the windows there are panoramic views of the wooded Simonside Hills and surrounding countryside, an area abounding in places of historical interest, nature trails, trout streams and good walking terrain. The hotel has a cosy bar, large lounge, television room and games rooms and the bedrooms, in the main building or skilfully converted from adjacent farm cottages, provide a high standard of comfort.

Nottinghamshire

LANGAR HALL,
Langar,
Nottinghamshire NG13 9HG

Tel: 0949 60559

Restaurant and residential licence; 9 bedrooms, all with private bathrooms; Historic interest; Children and dogs welcome; Car park (6); London 115 miles, Grantham 14, Nottingham 12.

Stuccoed and apricot washed, Langar Hall stands on an elevated site surveying the Vale of Belvoir. Built in 1830, it is the home of Imogen Skirving who welcomes up to six visitors at a time. Guests can, therefore, fully appreciate the style and atmosphere of country house living whilst enjoying the standards of a good hotel. Accommodation is in three suites, each of which has its own bathroom and one, the Brownlow Suite, has a four-poster bed. Dinner, featuring home-grown produce, is served in either the diningroom or the more formal pillared dininghall where a collection of nineteenth and twentieth century paintings are exhibited and are for sale. *ETB* 🌷🌷🌷.

UPTON FIELDS HOUSE,
Southwell,
Nottinghamshire ND25 0NG

Tel: 0636 812303

5 bedrooms, all with private bathrooms; Historic interest; Children over 5 years welcome; Car park (15); Nottingham 14 miles.

Upton Fields is a large country house situated on the outskirts of the small Minster town of Southwell. Set in its own one and a half acre garden, it is an attractive house with beautiful stained glass windows and magnificent inlaid galleried staircase. Five large bedrooms, en suite, with television and tea and coffee making facilities. All rooms have open country views yet are within easy reach of Nottingham, Newark, Sherwood and many beautiful gardens.

OLD ENGLAND HOTEL,
Sutton-on-Trent, Newark,
Nottinghamshire NG23 6QA

Tel: 0636 821216

Restaurant licence; 10 bedrooms, all with private facilities; Historic interest; Children and dogs welcome; Car park; London 133 miles, Nottingham 28, Newark-on-Trent 8.

Appropriately named, the Old England Hotel, owned and run by the Pike family for over fifty years, epitomises traditional hospitality, charm and courtesy, together with the modern amenities we expect from a first class establishment. All bedrooms are individually appointed with private facilities and the hotel is graced with a large collection of antique furniture delightfully displayed in its old-world setting. The menu too is selected from the very best of traditional fayre using locally produced meat and fresh vegetables. Extensive grounds invite the stroller and Sherwood Forest and Southwell Minster are readily accessible.

Oxfordshire

WHITE HART HOTEL,
High Street, Chipping Norton,
Oxfordshire OX7 5AD

Tel: 0608 2572

Licensed; 24 bedrooms, all with private bathrooms; Historic interest; Children welcome; Car park; Oxford 20 miles, Banbury 13.

The Inn was founded in the 13th century, during the reign of Richard II. Today, the inn houses an intriguing display of keepsakes and finds from its early history. A magnificent log fire dominates the White Hart's welcoming, stone-clad bar. Excellent meals are served in the spacious restaurant, where the cooking is tasty and distinctively Cotswold. Comfortably furnished and modernised throughout with the utmost discrimination, the inn offers impeccably appointed bedrooms, all with telephones, colour television, central heating and tea and coffee making equipment. Conference facilities also available.

RECOMMENDED SHORT-BREAK HOLIDAYS
IN BRITAIN

Introduced by John Carter, TV Holiday Expert and Journalist

Specifically designed to cater for the most rapidly growing sector of the holiday market in the UK. Illustrated details of hotels offering special 'Bargain Breaks' throughout the year.

Available from newsagents and bookshops or direct from the publishers:
£2.95 plus 30p postage.

FHG PUBLICATIONS LTD
Abbey Mill Business Centre, Seedhill,
Paisley, Renfrewshire PA1 1JN

THE PLOUGH AT CLANFIELD,
Bourton Road, Clanfield,
Oxfordshire OX8 2RB

Tel: 036-781 222/494

Licensed; 6 bedrooms, all with private bathrooms; Historic interest; Car park (35); Faringdon 4 miles.

Situated opposite the village green and built of Cotswold stone, The Plough has been described as the prettiest building within a 50-mile radius. Full of charm and character, the hotel has recently been refurbished throughout and under the personal direction of General Manager and Chef de Cuisine, Paul Barnard, the highest standards of comfort, service and cuisine are offered, all in keeping with the finest English traditions. Warm and hospitable in every respect, this recommended retreat lies in the heart of hunting country and is convenient for Cheltenham and Newbury racecourses. Magnificently appointed guest rooms will ensure sound repose and there is also a four-poster bedroom for the romantic.

LE MANOIR AUX QUAT'SAISONS,
Great Milton,
Oxfordshire OX9 7PD

Tel: 084-46 8881/2/3*

Licensed; 10 bedrooms, all with private bathrooms; Historic interest; Children over 7 welcome; Car park; Oxford 8 miles.

In rural seclusion yet only a short distance from the busy A40, this fine house has a long and fascinating history, the first traces of which appear in the 14th century although the present house was not built until more than a century later. Originally owned by a Norman nobleman, 'Le Manoir' has established connections with France and today this beautiful retreat is known internationally for its superb cuisine in the hands of Chef/Proprietor Raymond Blanc. The menus offer a stimulating selection of table d'hôte and à la carte dishes at lunchtime and in the evening, the impressive à la carte and Menu Gourmand comes into prominence — an unforgettable experience. Two intercommunicating dining rooms overlook the garden grounds which extend to 27 acres with a swimming pool, tennis court and water garden. The individually decorated bedrooms are indubitably in the luxury class and each has a spacious private bathroom, colour television and radio and some have a jacuzzi. The hotel has superb facilities for conferences and functions with secretarial services available. Special out-of-season midweek breaks offer great value.

REGENCY HOUSE,
River Terrace, Henley-on-Thames,
Oxfordshire RG9 1BG

Tel: 0491 571133

Residential licence; 5 bedrooms, all with private bathrooms; Historic interest; Children over 12 welcome; London 36 miles, Oxford 24, Reading 8.

Regency House is a riverside hotel in the heart of Henley-on-Thames, overlooking the Bridge and the famous Royal Regatta course beyond. Guests at this elegant establishment are promised personal service, with many thoughtful extras provided. All bedrooms are luxuriously appointed with private bathrooms, and most enjoy a spectacular river view. Colour television, coffee and tea making facilities, telephone and mini-bars are also provided. The Regency Supper Rooms offer the finest of English classical cooking. Regency House provides the ideal base for touring this beautiful area of England.

STUDLEY PRIORY HOTEL,
Horton-cum-Studley, Oxford,
Oxfordshire OX9 1AZ

Tel: 086-735 203

Licensed; 19 bedrooms, all with private bathrooms; Historic interest; Children welcome; Car park (100); Reading 26 miles.

By reason of its warm Cotswold stone and delightful setting, the Priory is imposing indeed, the very epitome of the grand and historic English country house. With its origins in the 12th century when it was a Benedictine nunnery, the building has changed little in exterior appearance since the days of Queen Elizabeth I. Converted into an hotel in 1961, the mellow rooms exude the friendliest of welcomes at the same time satisfying modern-day requirements. Guests are therefore assured of the best of contemporary comforts which blend in subtle fashion with the gracious aura of unhurried days long gone. Log fires in the main reception rooms and in the lovely oak-panelled bar augment the central heating. Bedrooms are furnished to the highest possible standards with private baths or showers, colour television, telephone and radio alarms as standard features. An Elizabethan suite with tester bed is available. Standing in 13 acres of wooded grounds and within easy reach of Oxford and numerous places of historic and rural interest, the hotel has exceptional facilities for conferences and receptions. Special interest/study weekends have been organised in recent years: subjects have included Wine, Fine Arts, Music, the Civil War and Historic Houses. Details of programmes planned for the near future are obtainable on request.

NOTE

All the information in this book is given in good faith in the belief that it is correct. However, the publishers cannot guarantee the facts given in these pages, neither are they responsible for changes in policy, ownership or terms that may take place after the date of going to press. Readers should always satisfy themselves that the facilities they require are available and that the terms, if quoted, still apply.

FALLOWFIELDS,
Kingston Bagpuize with Southmoor,
Oxfordshire OX13 5BH

Tel: 0865 820416*

Telex: 83388 Kings T.G. Att. Fallowfields

Residential licence; 4 bedrooms, 3 with private facilities; Historic interest; Children over 10 welcome, dogs by arrangement; Car park (15); Oxford 9 miles, Abingdon 6.

Surrounded by 12 acres of land including two acres of garden with Jacob sheep and horses, this interesting Gothic manor house is over 300 years old and welcomes visitors for bed and breakfast and evening dinner. The hotel specializes in excellent cuisine and makes full use of an exceptional variety of home grown vegetables and herbs. Personal service and attention is the keynote of Fallowfields and all bedrooms have tea and coffee making facilities, radio alarm, television and electric blankets. Croquet, outdoor heated swimming pool, hard tennis court and table tennis are available at the hotel and water sports, boating, fishing and golf are available nearby. Bed and breakfast from £21. *Recommended by The Guardian, Daily Telegraph, and Good Hotel Guide. BTA Commended.*

WESTWOOD COUNTRY HOTEL,
Hinksey Hill Top, Oxford,
Oxfordshire OX1 5BG

Tel: 0865 735408*

Restaurant and residential licence; 27 bedrooms, all with private bathrooms; Children welcome; Car park (40); Gloucester 49 miles, Reading 26.

The leafy grounds of this fine hotel are a bonus for nature lovers for the three acres are frequented by many species of birds, badgers, foxes, squirrels and even deer and are surrounded by a further 400 acres of woodland. The hotel itself was discovered to be frequented by astute tourists, many of whom return to sample again the excellent accommodation and superb cuisine. Single, double and family rooms all have private facilities, television, radio, baby-listening devices and tea and coffee-makers. A comfortable lounge with colour television is warmed by a log fire in winter and there is a convivial bar adjacent. Jacuzzi and mini-gym available free to guests. Good facilities exist for small conferences, meetings and weddings.

THE WELL HOUSE,
High Street, Watlington,
Oxfordshire

Tel: 049-161 3333

Restaurant and residential licence; 8 bedrooms, all with private bathrooms; Historic interest; Children welcome; Car park (15); Oxford 15 miles, Henley 9.

Nestling at the foot of the Chiltern Hills and in a conservation area, yet only two miles from the M40, The Well House has been part of this attractive old village for many years — indeed part of the hotel dates from the fifteenth century. Delicious restaurant meals are served daily both at lunchtimes and in the evening and bar meals are available by arrangement. The eight bedrooms are comfortably equipped and all have private bathrooms. For the active visitor squash and tennis can be arranged and there are many delightful walks, whilst for art lovers the glories of Oxford, Stonor Park, and Blenheim Palace are a short drive away. *ETB* 🌷 🌷 🌷 🌷.

Shropshire

THE OLD VICARAGE,
Church Lane, Baschurch,
Shropshire SY4 2EF

Tel: 0939 260135

Restaurant and residential licence; 7 bedrooms, all with private bathrooms; Historic interest; Children and dogs welcome; Car park (10); Shrewsbury 8 miles.

The Old Vicarage offers beautiful bedroom accommodation with en suite bathrooms, an elegant diningroom overlooking the extensive gardens and a comfortable lounge for the use of the residents. Each bedroom has been individually designed to create a superbly relaxed atmosphere and is equipped with a colour television, radio and tea/coffee making facilities. The Old Vicarage is set within two and a half acres of grounds, and within the village horse riding and grass tennis facilities are available, as well as a wild fowl pool.

THE REDFERN HOTEL,
Cleobury Mortimer,
Shropshire

Tel: 0299 270395 Telex: 335176

Licensed; 11 bedrooms, all with private bathrooms or showers; Children and dogs welcome; Car park; Ludlow 11 miles, Bewdley 8.

For centuries past travellers have stayed in the Shropshire market town of Cleobury Mortimer. Now a conservation area in the Rea Valley at the foot of Clee Hill (1750 feet) and on the edge of the Forest of Wyre, it forms a perfect centre for exploring the Welsh Marches with fine scenery and 2000 years of history. Ironbridge Industrial Museum, just 20 miles away, gives a fascinating insight into the Industrial Revolution, with many working machines and a Victorian pub. Acton Scott Farm Museum will take you back to the days of Shire horses and home-made butter, and a trip on the glorious Severn Valley Railway will conjure up images of long ago. After a day's adventuring, what better place to relax than in this warm and comfortable hotel, where good food, fine wines and friendly service will make your stay in Shropshire one to remember. All bedrooms have tea/coffee-making facilities, baby-listening, colour television, and telephone.

THE GLEBE FARM,
Diddlebury, Craven Arms,
Shropshire SY7 9DH
Tel: 058-476 221*

Residential and restaurant licence; 6 bedrooms, 2 with private bathrooms; Historic interest; Children over 10 welcome; Car park (10); Craven Arms 5 miles.

In glorious country surroundings on the Ludlow and Welsh border near Wenlock Edge, this is a charming working farm which offers wholesome and homely accommodation at extremely modest rates. Dating from Elizabethan days the farm, which is licensed, has a beautiful garden through which runs a gurgling stream and adjacent is the Saxon church of the tiny village of Diddlebury. All is peace and tranquillity; the perfect place for communion with nature and the restoration of jaded nerves. The house is friendly, warm and comfortable and Owners Eileen, Michael and Adrian Wilkes greet visitors as personal guests. Delicious farmhouse meals with a few surprises are served in a flagstoned and oak-beamed dining room and guest rooms, with or without private facilities, are handsomely equipped.

OVERTON GRANGE HOTEL,
Ludlow,
Shropshire
Tel: 0584 3500

Licensed; 17 bedrooms, 6 with private bathrooms; Children and dogs welcome; Car park; London 160 miles, Shrewsbury 29, Worcester 23, Hereford 22.

The beautiful and historic town of Ludlow has many places of interest, not least of which is its impressive 11th century castle overlooking the River Teme. The Edwardian mansion of Overton Grange is a recommended place in which to stay whilst undertaking a leisurely exploration of this delightful part of England. Its guest rooms are extremely well appointed, some with private baths or showers and most with colour television and panoramic views over the countryside. A comprehensive snack menu is available in a bar warmed by log fires and excellent table d'hôte and à la carte dishes are served in the oak-panelled restaurant. The Shropshire Hills are of great scenic beauty and the town also has a steeplechase course and 18-hole golf course.

SWEENEY HALL HOTEL,
Morda, Oswestry,
Shropshire SY10 9EU
Tel: 0691 652450

Licensed; 9 bedrooms, 6 with private bathrooms; Historic interest; Children and dogs welcome; Car park; Shrewsbury 16 miles.

Steeped in tradition and with elegant public rooms and superbly appointed guest rooms, this fine Georgian country house is set in its own 10 acres in the midst of extensive natural parkland. Only a short distance south of Oswestry, this is an excellent touring base for excursions into Wales and the historic border country; alternatively, one may enjoy the tranquillity of the lovely grounds where there is a putting green. Facilities for golf, shooting, fishing and riding exist nearby. The hotel offers a first-rate cuisine with much produce coming from the home garden. Both table d'hôte and à la carte menus are available.

---

* The appearance of an asterisk after the telephone number indicates that the hotel in question is closed for a period during the winter months. Exact dates should be ascertained from the hotel itself.

Somerset

CARNARVON ARMS HOTEL,
Dulverton,
Somerset TA22 9AE

Tel: 0398 23302*

Licensed; 25 bedrooms, all with private bathrooms; Children and dogs welcome; Car park; Exeter 27 miles, Taunton 26.

Close to the banks of the tinkling River Barle, this fine sporting hotel has some seven miles of salmon and trout fishing rights and other sporting activities available here include shooting, riding, swimming, tennis and croquet and there is also a well-equipped games room. Fifty acres of well-tended grounds offer peaceful relaxation against a backdrop of the richly wooded slopes of the Exmoor National Park. The comforts within this attractive hotel of late Victorian vintage are of a high order, the modern amenities blending happily with many fine antiques and open log fires. All the guest rooms have private bathrooms, colour televisions and telephones whilst the cuisine is traditionally English at its best and is supported by courteous service.

HORSINGTON HOUSE HOTEL,
Horsington, Templecombe,
Somerset BA8 0EG

Tel: 0963 70721

Licensed; 23 bedrooms, all with private bathrooms; Historic interest; Children and dogs welcome; Car park (50); London 115 miles, Bournemouth 40, Taunton 40, Bristol 35, Salisbury 30, Sherborne 9, Wincanton 3.

Built in the grand Georgian style, this magnificent house has many architectural delights, in particular the original oak staircase which forms the centrepiece of the foyer. One may consider the appetising possibilities of the superb table d'hôte and à la carte menus whilst enjoying an aperitif in the Old Music Room Bar. The cuisine is a revelation with several imaginative specialities to tempt the palate. Guest rooms are elegantly furnished and equipped with the finest modern appointments; each has its own bathroom or shower, radio, direct dial telephone, and colour television. The house is quietly set in seven acres of gardens incorporating a hard tennis court, croquet lawn, putting green and children's play area. Guests will receive a warm welcome from resident proprietors Judy and Robin Belcher. *AA**, RAC***, ETB* 🏵 🏵 🏵 🏵.

PHEASANT HOTEL,
Seavington St. Mary, Near Ilminster, Somerset

Tel: 0460 40502

Residential licence; 10 bedrooms, all with private bathrooms; Historic interest; Car park (60); Taunton 10 miles.

Waiting to serve travellers journeying to and from the West Country, this most attractive 17th century country hotel lies just off the main A303. Such is the excellence of the accommodation and services provided by the gifted Proprietors, Edmondo and Jacqueline Paoloni, that many guests make this their holiday choice. Luxuriously appointed and with carefully chosen water-colours adorning the walls, this efficient and friendly port of call has delightfully decorated guest rooms, each of which has a bathroom en suite, colour television and telephone. An appetising and imaginative selection of à la carte and table d'hôte dishes is on offer in the charming, old-world restaurant and there is a welcoming lounge bar with a large log fire.

PERITON PARK,
Middlecombe, Near Minehead, Somerset TA24 8SW

Tel: 0643 6885

Restaurant and residential licence; 7 bedrooms, 6 with private bathrooms; Historic interest; Dogs welcome; Car park; Taunton 24 miles.

A jewel set in grounds of 32 acres on the very fringe of the Exmoor National Park, this highly regarded country hotel is of direct appeal to those seeking escape from tedium and tribulation. The rewards here are legion with the salient practicalities being the superb Cordon Bleu cuisine with an Anglo-French flavour and superb accommodation. The warm and welcoming atmosphere of this handsome Victorian house is captured in its delightful lounges with fine furnishings, books and open fires, whilst guest rooms are beautifully appointed in individual style; most have en suite bathrooms, television, telephone, radio. Full English breakfast is served in the bedrooms. Facilities include a billiard room and horse riding for experienced riders.

NOTE

All the information in this book is given in good faith in the belief that it is correct. However, the publishers cannot guarantee the facts given in these pages, neither are they responsible for changes in policy, ownership or terms that may take place after the date of going to press. Readers should always satisfy themselves that the facilities they require are available and that the terms, if quoted, still apply.

YEW TREE COUNTRY HOUSE,
Sand, Wedmore,
Somerset

Tel: 0934 712520

Licensed; 5 bedrooms, all with private bathrooms; Historic interest; Children welcome; Car park; M5 Junction 22, 6 miles, Cheddar 4.

A delightful eighteenth century country house set in two acres of grounds in the charming Somerset hamlet of Sand. Yew Tree Country House has been sympathetically modernised to retain the finest of period features combined with the comforts of the new. Accommodation is of a high standard, with en suite facilities, colour TV, and tea and coffee making. Superb English and Continental dishes are offered in the restaurant, complemented by a good range of wines. This is an ideal area for country and field sports, and there are many places of interest to visit nearby: Wells, Glastonbury, and Cheddar are in easy reach, and the Georgian village of Wedmore is one mile away. Winter Breaks available. Visa and Access cards accepted. *ETB* 🌸🌸🌸.

DANESWOOD HOUSE HOTEL,
Shipham, Near Cheddar,
Somerset BS25 1RD

Tel: 093-484 3145

Licensed; 13 bedrooms, 8 with private bathroms; Children over 12 years welcome; Car park (30), garages (5); Wells 12 miles.

The luxurious accommodation here includes a honeymoon suite with 7ft. bed and large bathroom with sunken bath. All other guest rooms are individually decorated to a high standard with colour television and central heating and many have en suite facilities and panoramic views. Built in the Edwardian era as a health hydro, the hotel has been transformed into a charming country house hotel combining excellent modern amenities with its original elegant character. High up in the Mendips and only two miles from Cheddar Caves, the hotel has comfortable lounges and a well-stocked bar. The English and Continental cuisine is interesting, varied, carefully-planned and delightfully presented. *AA***

SIMONSBATH HOUSE HOTEL,
Simonsbath, Near Minehead,
Somerset TA24 7SH

Tel: 064-383 259*

Residential and restaurant licence; 7 bedrooms, all with private bathrooms; Historic interest; Children over 10 welcome; Car park; Exeter 55 miles, Barnstaple 21, Lynton 7.

Beautifully furnished with an eye to colour and style, this interesting house is one of the oldest in the Exmoor National Park having been built in 1654 immediately after the Civil War. The aura of its aristocratic past is retained by four-poster beds, velvet drapes and fine oak-panelling. Later a hunting lodge of the Fortescue family, this noble building is now a comfortable hotel offering a high standard of accommodation and generous, fresh home-cooked food. An excellent centre for walking, hunting, fishing or touring holidays, the house is surrounded by beautiful valleys and is within easy driving distance of Dunkery Beacon, the Doone Valley, Dunster and the coast.

RALEIGH MANOR,
Wheddon Cross,
Somerset TA24 7BB

Tel: 064-384 484*

Residential and restaurant licence; 7 bedrooms, all with private bathrooms; Children over 8 and dogs welcome; Car park (10); Exeter 37 miles, Minehead 9.

With its very name ringing with historic significance, this elegant late-Victorian manor house stands 1000 feet high in the Exmoor National Park overlooking Snowdrop Valley, the Bristol Channel and the coast of Wales beyond. A country house hotel since 1980, Raleigh Manor has been delightfully furnished in period style, including a half-tester bed in the Squire's Bedroom and log fires to enhance the welcoming atmosphere. Guests may rest assured in more ways than one for skilfully introduced modern innovations include central heating, bedrooms with private bathroom, colour television and tea and coffee-making facilities. A varied menu provides a tempting selection of home-cooked dishes. Riding and fishing may be arranged locally.

* The appearance of an asterisk after the telephone number indicates that the hotel in question is closed for a period during the winter months. Exact dates should be ascertained from the hotel itself.

WESTERCLOSE COUNTRY HOUSE HOTEL,
Withypool,
Somerset TA24 7QR
Tel: 064-383 302*

Residential and restaurant licence; 11 bedrooms, all with private bathrooms; Children and dogs welcome; Car park (12); Exford 2 miles.

Nestling in a charming village in the heart of Exmoor, this attractive little hotel will appeal to lovers of heather-clad hills, wooded valleys and abundant wild life. What is more, the free fresh air will sharpen the appetite and guests may look forward to excellent traditional fare with the emphasis on local produce. Westerclose is warm and welcoming with a cosy lounge and comfortable bedrooms, all of which have private bathrooms and superb views. Moods active and passive are well catered for. There is much to explore in the neighbourhood and the house, which stands in grounds of nine acres, has its own stables. Hunting, shooting and fishing may all be enjoyed locally. *AA**, RAC**; ETB* 🌷 🌷 🌷.

FENNY CASTLE HOUSE HOTEL,
Fenny Castle, Wookey, Near Wells,
Somerset BA5 1NN
Tel: 0749 72265

Residential and restaurant licence; 3 bedrooms, all with private bathrooms; Historic interest; Children over 12 welcome; Car park (60); Bristol 21 miles, Glastonbury 6.

In a riverside setting amidst 60 acres of beautiful countryside, this lovely Queen Anne house overlooks the historic and mysterious earthworks of Fenny Castle, one-time outpost in the Anglo-Saxon War. There is nothing mysterious, however, about the warmth of welcome modern-day guests receive at this comfortable retreat. Accommodation is limited but nonetheless of the highest order, rooms being delightfully furnished and appointed. Log fires augment the central heating in cooler weather and the elegant restaurant offers a wide variety of English and French dishes and a selection of choice wines. There are two fine lounges, both of which have far-reaching views over the Somerset levels. First-class facilities for conferences exist here.

> * The appearance of an asterisk after the telephone number indicates that the hotel in question is closed for a period during the winter months. Exact dates should be ascertained from the hotel itself.

Staffordshire

BUTTERTON MOOR COUNTRY HOUSE,
Parson's Lane, Butterton, Near Leek, Staffordshire ST13 7PD

Tel: 053-88 289

Licensed; 11 bedrooms, all with private bathrooms; Historic interest; Children and dogs welcome; Car park (20); Leek 6 miles.

In a superb setting in the Peak District National Park is this delightful eighteenth century country house standing in its own 11 acre grounds. Butterton Moor is an ideal spot for a quiet retreat for reflection and relaxation, and hosts Marion and Kevin Squire do everything to ensure that guests feel welcome. Food is excellent, and there is a drinks service for guests. All bedrooms are comfortably furnished, with en suite facilities and tea and coffee makers. The house itself retains all its original charm, with exposed beams and open fires throughout. There are leisure activities available nearby, while Alton Towers, the Manifold Valley, and Dovedale are conveniently close. *ETB* 🏵 🏵 🏵.

Please mention
Recommended COUNTRY HOTELS
when seeking refreshment or
accommodation at a Hotel
mentioned in these pages

DOG AND PARTRIDGE HOTEL, Tutbury, Staffordshire

Tel: 0283 813030

Licensed; 17 bedrooms, all with private bathrooms; Historic interest; Car park (80); London 124 miles, Burton-upon-Trent 4.

Built in the late fourteenth century and mentioned in Domesday Book, the inn, beautifully timbered, first came into prominence through bull running and later as a coaching house. The restaurant is of justifiable repute specialising in French cuisine. There are three bars, a wine bar carvery serving hot and cold food, and music on the grand piano nightly. Bedrooms are of the highest standard; all have private bath/ shower, colour television, radio alarm and mini-bar. *British Tourist Authority Commended Country Hotel.*

FOR THE MUTUAL GUIDANCE OF GUEST AND HOST

Every year literally thousands of holidays, short-breaks and overnight stops are arranged through our guides, the vast majority without any problems at all. In a handful of cases, however, difficulties do arise about bookings, which often could have been prevented from the outset.

It is important to remember that when accommodation has been booked, both parties — guests and hosts — have entered into a form of contract. We hope that the following points will provide helpful guidance.

GUESTS: When enquiring about accommodation, be as precise as possible. Give exact dates, numbers in your party and the ages of any children. State the number and type of rooms wanted and also what catering you require — bed and breakfast, full board, etc. Make sure that the position about evening meals is clear — and about pets, reductions for children or any other special points.

Read our reviews carefully to ensure that the proprietors you are going to contact can supply what you want. Ask for a letter confirming all arrangements, if possible.

If you have to cancel, do so as soon as possible. Proprietors do have the right to retain deposits and under certain circumstances to charge for cancelled holidays if adequate notice is not given and they cannot re-let the accommodation.

HOSTS: Give details about your facilities and about any special conditions. Explain your deposit system clearly and arrangements for cancellations, charges, etc, and whether or not your terms include VAT.

If for any reason you are unable to fulfil an agreed booking without adequate notice, you may be under an obligation to arrange alternative suitable accommodation or to make some form of compensation.

While every effort is made to ensure accuracy, we regret that FHG Publications cannot accept responsibility for errors, omissions or misrepresentation in our entries or any consequences thereof. Prices in particular should be checked because we go to press early. We will follow up complaints but cannot act as arbiters or agents for either party.

Suffolk

CONEY WESTON HALL COUNTRY HOUSE HOTEL,
Coney Weston, Bury St. Edmunds,
Suffolk IP31 1HG
Tel: 035-921 441

Residential and restaurant licence; 7 bedrooms, 4 with private bathrooms; Historic interest; Car park; Bury St. Edmunds 12 miles.

Surrounded by the farmlands of the Norfolk/Suffolk border and set in 25 acres of its own gardens and parkland, Coney Weston Hall is a fine country house dating from the Queen Anne period. Guests have use of an elegant drawing room, library and second sitting room. Most bedrooms are en suite and there is central heating throughout, supplemented by log fires in winter. Outside is a heated swimming pool. However, it is in the culinary department that the hotel really comes into its own. David Backhouse, the proprietor, is an authority on food and his own farm supplies the hotel with produce grown without the use of chemical fertilisers. The menu is prepared with great care to ensure a selection that offers a variety of complementary flavours and includes vegetarian dishes.

CEDARS HOTEL,
Needham Road, Stowmarket,
Suffolk IP14 2AJ
Tel: 0449 612668*

Licensed; 20 bedrooms, 18 with private bathrooms; Historic interest; Children welcome; Car park (70); Ipswich 12 miles.

The incursion into a touring area that is, at last, gaining in popularity, brought us to the outskirts of the pleasant little town of Stowmarket where the timbers and stonework of this delightful hotel give a clue to its 16th century origins as a farmhouse. Now offering an impressive range of hotel, restaurant and function facilities, The Cedars is conveniently near Ipswich, Harwich and Felixstowe. Most of the bedrooms (some on the ground-floor) have bathrooms en suite, colour television, radio and tea and coffee-makers. With an appetising selection of light meals, the welcoming bar also proves a good meeting place prior to a visit to the charming restaurant where an extensive choice of à la carte dishes will certainly tempt the palate. Special rates are available for weekend breaks which represent very good value for money.

SECKFORD HALL HOTEL,
Woodbridge,
Suffolk IP13 6NU

Tel: 0394 385678

Licensed; 24 bedrooms, all with private bathrooms, 4 four-posters; Historic interest; Children and dogs welcome; Car park (100), garages (3); London 80 miles, Norwich 48, Aldeburgh 17, Saxmundham 13, Ipswich 8.

This splendid creeper-clad country house epitomises the unhurried grace of medieval Tudor England. Indeed, built in 1530, Seckford Hall is one of our finest examples of Tudor architecture. The Great Hall is now a lounge and bedrooms have individual colour schemes and appointments of the highest standard including radio, colour television, teletext and tea and coffee making facilities; amongst them is a superb four-poster bedroom dating from 1587. The diningroom is resplendent with monastic oak panelling and, backed by unobtrusive service, one may enjoy a wide range of well-presented dishes. The house speciality is locally caught lobster and the enormously attractive lobster pond in the hall makes an interesting feature. Park-like grounds surround the house and from the terrace garden there are views across a lake; this is a tranquil spot in which to relax. Look out for the hotel sign on the A12 Woodbridge by-pass. *Egon Ronay and Derek Johansen recommended. ETB* 🌷 🌷 🌷 🌷.

Other specialised

FHG PUBLICATIONS

* Recommended SHORT-BREAK HOLIDAYS IN BRITAIN   £2.95

* Recommended WAYSIDE INNS OF BRITAIN   £2.95

* PETS WELCOME!   £1.95

* BED AND BREAKFAST IN BRITAIN   £1.95

Published annually. Please add 30p postage (U.K. only) when ordering from the publishers:

FHG PUBLICATIONS LTD
Abbey Mill Business Centre, Seedhill,
Paisley, Renfrewshire PA1 1JN

Surrey

PENNYHILL PARK HOTEL & COUNTRY CLUB,
College Ride, Bagshot,
Surrey GU19 5ET
Tel: 0276 71774

Licensed; 48 bedrooms, all with private bathrooms; Historic interest; Children welcome, dogs by arrangement; Car park (250); Basingstoke 21 miles, Windsor 11.

This stately English Country Manor House, nestling on the Surrey-Berkshire border, is today a haven of unexpected calm from the bustle of central London just 27 miles away. At Pennyhill Park we play host to those who treasure privacy and quiet. The house is situated in 112 acres of estate including landscaped gardens, stunning parkland and a trout lake — to be enjoyed whatever the season. It also offers every modern amenity including Country Club, swimming pool, nine-hole golf course, horse riding, and clay pigeon shooting. There are just 48 exclusive rooms and suites. Each room is furnished and decorated using soft, elegant fabrics and comforting themes such as 'walnut' and 'oak'. As with everything else, the staff at Pennyhill Park care about the way they prepare and present the food which is served in the splendour of the Latymer Restaurant.

PLEASE ENCLOSE A STAMPED
ADDRESSED ENVELOPE WHEN
WRITING TO ENQUIRE ABOUT
ACCOMMODATION FEATURED IN
THIS GUIDE

SELSDON PARK HOTEL,
Sanderstead, South Croydon,
Surrey CR2 8YA

Tel: 01-657 8811 Telex: 945003

*Licensed; 7 suites; 130 twin/double-bedded rooms; 45 single, all with private bathrooms;
Historic interest; Children welcome; Car park (200); Gatwick 15 miles, London 13, Croydon 3.*

Did you realise that just 30 minutes from London, set amid the Surrey Hills in 200 acres of magnificent parkland, is situated Selsdon Park, undoubtedly one of England's most exquisite country house hotels, with a long history that dates back to Saxon times? Now, over a thousand years later, all the advantages of the twentieth century are utilised to the full, providing superb facilities together with a tradition of personal service that gives the hotel a unique and friendly atmosphere. Each bedroom has a private bathroom and colour television while the list of amenities available to residents includes: tropical leisure complex, championship 18-hole golf course, hard and grass tennis courts, open-air heated swimming pool, four full-sized billiard tables and a dinner-dance every Saturday. A delightful and relaxing holiday or a weekend break can be enjoyed with up to 40% reduction for children under 12. Personal attention is given by an experienced and professional management team under the direction of the Resident Proprietor, Mr Basil Sanderson, FHCIMA. Colour brochure and tariff are available on request. *AA, RAC****, ETB* 🌷🌷🌷🌷.

East Sussex

CALAHONDA HOTEL,
Cooden Beach, Near Bexhill-on-Sea, Sussex (East) TN39 4TX

Tel: 042-43 5405*

Residential licence; 3 bedrooms, all with private bathrooms; Car park (6); London 66 miles, Eastbourne 10, Bexhill-on-Sea 2.

Standing in a sheltered bay in one of the finest positions on the South Coast is this delightful little hotel where quality rather than quantity is the hallmark. Guests are assured of the finest of personal attention at all times from resident proprietors Mr. and Mrs. Grinham, who make every effort to ensure that your stay is a memorable one. Calahonda has three suites, each individually furnished and decorated throughout, and guests can enjoy sea views of the English Channel and Pevensey Bay or country vistas of the Pevensey Marshes and the Sussex Downs from their windows. The diningroom also displays the high standards found throughout, with full use made of local produce and food graced with silver service, cut glass, and Royal Worcester china. Calahonda stands at the heart of one of the most beautiful and unspoilt areas in England, and it makes a tranquil base from which to explore the delights of the South Coast with its historic sites, National Trust walks and sporting facilities and the Downs with their rolling, grassy hills and tiny, centuries-old, unspoilt villages. *ETB* 🌸 🌸 🌸 🌸.

RECOMMENDED SHORT-BREAK HOLIDAYS
IN BRITAIN

Introduced by John Carter, TV Holiday Expert and Journalist

Specifically designed to cater for the most rapidly growing sector of the holiday market in the UK. Illustrated details of hotels offering special 'Bargain Breaks' throughout the year.

Available from newsagents and bookshops or direct from the publishers:
£2.95 plus 30p postage.

FHG PUBLICATIONS LTD
Abbey Mill Business Centre, Seedhill,
Paisley, Renfrewshire PA1 1JN

BEAUPORT PARK HOTEL,
Near Hastings,
Sussex (East)
Tel: 0424 51222

Licensed; 16 double bedrooms, 7 single, all with bathrooms; Car park; Battle 3 miles. Hastings 3.

This fine three-star country house hotel, set amidst 33 acres of woodland and picturesque formal gardens offers old fashioned personal service from resident directors Kenneth and Helena Melsom. All guest rooms have private bathrooms and are equipped with remote control colour television, electric trouser press, auto dial telephone, hairdryer and tea/coffee making facilities. There is a heated swimming pool in the grounds, country walks, tennis courts, croquet lawn and a putting green, with an 18-hole golf course, riding stables and squash courts adjoining. Prospective guests are invited to write or telephone for brochure and tariff, and a country house bargain breaks leaflet. 'Country House Getaway Breaks' are available all year.

HORSTED PLACE,
Little Horsted, Near Uckfield,
East Sussex TN22 5TS
Tel: 0825 75581*

Restaurant and residential licence; 17 bedrooms, all with private bathrooms; Historic interest; Children over 7 years; Car park (30); Uckfield 2 miles.

The soaring gables and chimneys of this grand country house reach as high as the impressive hospitality and impeccable service it promotes. Representing the very essence of elegant luxury, the facilities here are of the highest order from the delightfully furnished reception rooms to the sumptuous guest suites, all of which are individually styled with panache and an eye for harmony and colour. With their own sitting area, these rooms enjoy panoramic views of the gardens and countryside and provide the ultimate in comfort. Fine pictures adorn the walls and it is even a pleasure to stroll down the hallway. One dines 'par excellence' in the magnificent Pugin diningroom to the accompaniment of porcelain, silver and spotless napery. Dishes portray a desire for the creative and much pride is taken in presentation with wines to complement every taste. Recreational diversions at Horsted also have a wide appeal with an all-weather hard tennis court and indoor heated swimming pool to absorb surplus energy as well as the more gentle pleasures of the croquet lawn or merely strolling through the enchanting gardens. Happily placed between London and the south coast, this highly recommended retreat has superb facilities for conferences, board meetings and private functions.

LITTLE ORCHARD HOUSE,
West Street, Rye,
Sussex (East) TN31 7ES

Tel: 0797 223831

3 bedrooms, all with private bathrooms; Historic interest; London 67 miles, Canterbury 33, Battle 14, Tenterden 12.

Rye is the most complete small medieval hill town in Britain, and this charming Georgian townhouse is a delightful surprise right at the heart of the Ancient Town, quietly situated in the picturesque cobbled streets with a traditional walled old English garden and its unique Smugglers Watch Tower. Each bedroom is decorated to an individual theme and has a bathroom en suite. Paintings and old prints are displayed throughout the house which is stylishly decorated and furnished with antiques. Visitors will enjoy a generous country breakfast and with at least five outstanding restaurants within walking distance you will be spoilt for choice in the evenings. Table reservations will gladly be made on your behalf. *BTA Commended; ETB* ♛ ♛ ♛.

West Sussex

HOWARDS HOTEL,
Crossbush, Arundel,
Sussex (West) BN18 9PQ

Tel: 0903 882655

Licensed; 10 bedrooms, all with private bathrooms; Car park (100); Chichester 11 miles.

Gazing across parkland towards Arundel Castle, only a medieval stone's throw away, Howards is obviously popular with family parties and the excellent luncheons and 6-course dinners served in the bistro-style Cafe des Amis excited much favourable comment. The traditional Sunday dinner is a fun occasion for all with reduced rate menus and free fun packs for children. The Carvery, spared the enthusiasm of young children, also provides superb fare in quieter surroundings. There is a warmly welcoming bar where hot and cold meals are dispensed daily. Those constrained to stay at this fine hotel will find delightfully decorated guest rooms, all equipped with private bathrooms, colour television and direct-dial telephone.

AVISFORD PARK COUNTRY HOTEL,
Walberton, Arundel,
Sussex (West) BN18 0LS

Tel: 0243 551215

Licensed; 100 bedrooms, all with private bathrooms; Historic interest; Children and dogs welcome; Car park (120); Brighton 21 miles, Chichester 11.

Released from its duties as a boys' school in 1974 and now one of the finest country hotels in Britain, Avisford Park has a handsome facade that hides modern amenities of the very highest quality. Magnificent leisure facilities exist within the 40-acre grounds, including a 9-hole golf course, squash, tennis (March-October), putting, croquet, indoor and outdoor swimming pools, sauna and snooker room. Indeed, there is no need to leave the premises to enjoy a memorable holiday and the cuisine in the Cedar Room may be understated as superb. However, with Goodwood, Fontwell Park, the Sussex coast and so many places of interest nearby, it would take a stay of some months to take in all these pleasures. Guests, albeit restricted to a shorter visit, will be enchanted with the accommodation with comfortable, well-furnished public rooms and bedrooms all having bathroom en suite, colour television, radio, telephone and tea tray. The hotel is a popular venue for private functions with several rooms available, including the splendid ballroom.

MILL HOUSE HOTEL,
Ashington,
Sussex (West)

Tel: 0903 892426

Residential and restaurant licence; 11 bedrooms, 9 with private bathrooms; Historic interest; Children and dogs welcome; Car park (15); Horsham 12 miles, Worthing 9.

Verdant West Sussex incorporates many places of natural and sporting interest and there can be few better venues to choose as a base than this delightful small country house hotel. The house reposes in a quiet situation, just off the main A24 about halfway between Horsham and Worthing. Peter and Jan Bench ensure that, with personal attention, the old-world atmosphere engendered by this comfortably furnished retreat complements its noteworthy, reasonably-priced cuisine and willing service. Guest rooms provide modern amenities, including colour television and direct dial telephones, and there is a restful lounge and cocktail bar in which to while away unhurried moments. Weekend Breaks are offered all year round.

HICKSTEAD RESORT HOTEL,
Bolney,
Sussex (West)   Tel: 044-46 48023

Licensed; 49 bedrooms, all with private bathrooms; Children welcome; Car park (100); London 52 miles, Haywards Heath 6.

The Hickstead Resort Hotel is set in 7 acres of grounds overlooking the South Downs, situated only 15 miles from Gatwick Airport. The newly built guest bedrooms comprise comfortable rooms with en suite facilities, colour television, tea and coffee making facilities, trouser press and hairdryer. The Sussex Gate Restaurant offers classical French and modern English cuisine, served in a country house atmosphere. Bar snacks available in the Grange Bar at lunch only. The health club comprises a heated indoor pool, sauna, jacuzzi and solarium. *RAC, AA***; ETB* 👑 👑 👑 👑.

BURPHAM COUNTRY HOTEL,
Old Down, Burpham, Near Arundel,
Sussex (West) BN18 9RJ   Tel: 0903 882160

Residential and restaurant licence; 10 bedrooms, 9 with private bathrooms; Historic interest; Children over 12 welcome; Car park; Brighton 21 miles, Chichester 11.

Reputed to have been a hunting lodge of the Duke of Norfolk in earlier times, this charming country hotel has been carefully restored to its original elegance and splendour and now offers all the comforts and amenities demanded by present-day visitors. Privately owned and run, Burpham Country Hotel is situated in one of the most peaceful and unspoilt villages in West Sussex with superb views over the South Downs. Bedrooms are spacious and well furnished, each having colour television and tea-making facilities, while the restaurant offers both table d'hôte and à la carte menus with vegetarian dishes included. Arundel Wildfowl Trust, Brighton, Worthing, Chichester and Goodwood are all within easy reach.

NOTE

All the information in this book is given in good faith in the belief that it is correct. However, the publishers cannot guarantee the facts given in these pages, neither are they responsible for changes in policy, ownership or terms that may take place after the date of going to press. Readers should always satisfy themselves that the facilities they require are available and that the terms, if quoted, still apply.

WOODSTOCK HOUSE HOTEL,
Charlton, Near Chichester,
Sussex (West) PO18 0HU

Tel: 024-363 666

Restaurant and residential licence; 11 bedrooms, 9 with private facilities; Historic interest; Children over 12 years welcome; Car park (12); Chichester 6 miles, Goodwood 1.

Woodstock House Hotel, once closely associated with the premier hunt of England, is situated in one of the most picturesque valleys in West Sussex, between Chichester and Midhurst. There is an inner courtyard garden with fish pond and conservatory which is overlooked by a balconied sun terrace. Inside is an intimate cocktail bar and luxurious lounge with log fires. Excellent food at reasonable prices is served in a secluded candlelit restaurant. Nigel and Fiona are always available to give their personal attention. Guest rooms are all individually decorated, including a four poster bedroom, and have modern amenities including colour television and tea making facilities. Ideally placed for horse racing, golf and much more.

SOUTH LODGE,
Lower Beeding,
Sussex (West) RH13 6PS

Tel: 040-376-711

Licensed; 39 bedrooms, all with private bathrooms; Historic interest; Children and dogs welcome; Car park; Horsham 4 miles.

A private family home in late-Victorian days, this beautifully-restored house stands in 90 acres of gardens and parkland created by the original owner, the noted botanist and explorer, Lord Frederick Du Cane Godman. Now a splendid country hotel noted for its fine cuisine, South Lodge has elegant and comfortable rooms, including a library and magnificent lounge with open fires, ornamental ceilings and oak-panelling contributing greatly to the ambience. Guest rooms are individually furnished and spacious; all have private bathrooms, colour television and direct-dial telephone, whilst the majority enjoy far-reaching views of the Sussex countryside. The grounds provide opportunities for such activities as horse riding, tennis, croquet, clay pigeon shooting and trout fishing.

CHEQUERS HOTEL,
Church Place, Pulborough,
Sussex (West) RH20 1AD

Tel: 079-82 2486

Residential and restaurant licence; 9 bedrooms, all with private bathrooms; Historic interest; Children and dogs welcome; Car park (14); London 49 miles, Bognor Regis 17, Horsham 13.

Tastefully extended over the years, this original Queen Anne house huddles on the edge of Pulborough village gazing peacefully out over the Arun Valley to the South Downs beyond. Excellent home-cooked dishes using local produce and fresh vegetables has given Chequers its reputation for fine cuisine, and proprietors Mr and Mrs Searancke ensure that all special diets will be catered for with willing cheerfulness. Guest accommodation is comfortable and well appointed, and open fires make this as pleasant a holiday venue in winter as it is in summer when the garden is bright with colour. Bargain breaks are available throughout the year. *RAC**; ETB* 🌷 🌷 🌷.

FOR THE MUTUAL GUIDANCE
OF GUEST AND HOST

Every year literally thousands of holidays, short-breaks and overnight stops are arranged through our guides, the vast majority without any problems at all. In a handful of cases, however, difficulties do arise about bookings, which often could have been prevented from the outset.

It is important to remember that when accommodation has been booked, both parties — guests and hosts — have entered into a form of contract. We hope that the following points will provide helpful guidance.

GUESTS: When enquiring about accommodation, be as precise as possible. Give exact dates, numbers in your party and the ages of any children. State the number and type of rooms wanted and also what catering you require — bed and breakfast, full board, etc. Make sure that the position about evening meals is clear — and about pets, reductions for children or any other special points.

Read our reviews carefully to ensure that the proprietors you are going to contact can supply what you want. Ask for a letter confirming all arrangements, if possible.

If you have to cancel, do so as soon as possible. Proprietors do have the right to retain deposits and under certain circumstances to charge for cancelled holidays if adequate notice is not given and they cannot re-let the accommodation.

HOSTS: Give details about your facilities and about any special conditions. Explain your deposit system clearly and arrangements for cancellations, charges, etc, and whether or not your terms include VAT.

If for any reason you are unable to fulfil an agreed booking without adequate notice, you may be under an obligation to arrange alternative suitable accommodation or to make some form of compensation.

While every effort is made to ensure accuracy, we regret that FHG Publications cannot accept responsibility for errors, omissions or misrepresentation in our entries or any consequences thereof. Prices in particular should be checked because we go to press early. We will follow up complaints but cannot act as arbiters or agents for either party.

Warwickshire

BILLESLEY MANOR,
Billesley, Alcester, Near Stratford-upon-Avon, Warwickshire B49 6NF

Tel: 0789 763737

Licensed; 41 bedrooms, all with private bathrooms; Historic interest; Children welcome; Car park; Warwick 15 miles, Stratford-upon-Avon 7.

This is a house of most pleasing aspect and on stepping into the reception lounge, one is immediately made aware of a standard of luxurious well-being by the elegant Louis XIV furniture. Further acquaintance will reveal that an eye for colour and style has maintained hotel facilities that would be hard to better and with more than a pinch of intriguing history thrown in. Four-poster beds are commonplace and the Shakespeare Room has a bathroom with gold-plated fittings — to some, the ultimate in luxury. Reference books say Will wrote 'As You Like It' in this very room, presumably before the gold-plated era! A trapdoor in a cupboard leads to a priests' hiding place. There are two superb oak-panelled restaurants and one may dine memorably with silver cutlery and hand-cut glassware complementing the excellent cuisine. For those fearful that these facilities may be ostentatious, it should be stressed that a homely atmosphere prevails throughout and service is friendly and efficient. Bedrooms are tastefully furnished and have been fitted out with spacious bathrooms, colour television, direct-dial telephone and trouser presses. In the 11 acres of well-kept grounds are two tennis courts, a heated swimming pool and croquet lawn.

MOXHULL HALL HOTEL,
Holly Lane, Wishaw, Sutton Coldfield, Warwickshire B76 9PE

Tel: 021-329 2056

Licensed; 21 bedrooms, all with private bathrooms; Historic interest; Children and dogs welcome; Car park; London 107 miles, Birmingham 7.

Built at some expense at the turn of the century and now a country hotel of great presence, Moxhull Hall has a wealth of architectural attractions, of particular note being a magnificent carved oak staircase taken from Kenilworth Castle and the fine dark oak panelling in the dining room. Extensive gardens and woodland surround the hotel and it is hard to believe that the centre of Birmingham is only seven miles away. Lovers of good food foregather here from all parts of the Midlands to enjoy the excellence of the English and French cuisine. Making fullest use of the recommended facilities here, guests may relax in beautifully appointed rooms, all fitted with private bath or shower, colour television, radio and telephone.

Wiltshire

THE RUDLOE PARK HOTEL AND RESTAURANT,
Leafy Lane, Corsham,
Wiltshire SN13 0PA

Tel: 0225 810555

Residential and restaurant licence; 11 bedrooms, all with private bathrooms; Historic interest; Children over 10 welcome; Car park (100); Chippenham 4 miles.

Originally the home of the family who made their fortune from quarrying the world famous Portland stone this fine old building is now run as a peaceful country house hotel under the capable and caring supervision of hosts Ian and Marion Overend. The elegant dining room overlooks the gardens and provides a most congenial setting for the enjoyment of one's choice from the excellent table d'hôte or à la carte menus both at luncheon and in the evening. The bedrooms, too, are luxuriously appointed (some with four poster beds) and capture the grace and charm of a bygone era. The Rudloe Park is recommended by Egon Ronay, Ashley Courtenay and Michelin and enjoys three star rating from the AA and RAC. Signpost Food, Wine and Garden Awards.

CRUDWELL COURT HOTEL,
Crudwell, Near Malmesbury,
Wiltshire SN16 9EP

Tel: 06667 7194/7195

Restaurant and residential licence; 15 bedrooms, all with private bathrooms; Historic interest; Children and dogs welcome; Car park (35); Cheltenham 20 miles, Bath 20, exit 17 M4 7, Cirencester 5, Malmesbury 3.

A recently refurbished seventeenth century vicarage set in three acres of lovely Cotswold walled gardens, with lily ponds and a heated swimming pool. The garden gate leads to a Saxon village church. The resident owners have created a relaxed and comfortable country house atmosphere, with log fires, excellent cooking and fine wines. The 14 bedrooms are spacious and individually decorated to a high standard with private bathrooms, and lovely views of the surrounding garden. All cooking is freshly prepared to order by the owner chef, with vegetables from the hotel's own garden. The panelled diningroom is open to non-residents. Preferential rates for mid-week bookings and weekends off season. Special Christmas package.

IVY HOUSE HOTEL,
Marlborough,
Wiltshire SN8 1HJ

Tel: 0672 55333

Restaurant licence; 35 bedrooms, all with private bathrooms; Historic interest; Children over 12 welcome, dogs by arrangement; Car park (30); Chippenham 19 miles, Swindon 12.

This charming Grade II listed Georgian building, adjoining the High Street of mellow Marlborough, was something of a surprise. Built in 1707 and in turn a boys' school and coaching inn, it has recently undergone skilful refurbishment and extension and now offers luxurious accommodation in the modern idiom both in the main hotel and new Beeches wing, each guest room having bathroom en suite, colour television, in-house video and direct-dial telephone, plus several useful extras. Reception rooms, cocktail bar and Garden Restaurant are delightfully furnished, the latter splendidly effective in pink and blue Palladian style. The enthusiasm of the catering staff was plainly evident in the excellent cuisine and the hotel is justly popular for conferences and functions.

BISHOPSTROW HOUSE,
Warminster,
Wiltshire BA12 9HH

Tel: 0935 212312

Restaurant and residential licence; 28 bedrooms, all with private bathrooms; Historic interest; Car park (35); Bath 18 miles.

Walk or drive through the wrought-iron gates of this beautiful Georgian mansion, gaze at the warm stone facade and step into the central hall and a world of ordered elegance. An hotel since 1978, Bishopstrow House is magnificently furnished with spacious rooms all grace and favour and everything in its place. Luxuriously appointed guest rooms, each with bathroom, colour television and telephone and magnificent suites with their own jacuzzi whirlpools, are reached via a grand staircase and, on all sides, antique furniture and oil paintings add to the rich atmosphere with log fires adding warmth. The surroundings of the house are well in keeping with the aesthetic pleasures within, with indoor and outdoor swimming pools and tennis courts, whilst the parklike grounds leading down to the River Wylye feature an impressive pillared temple and ornamental trees. The hotel has a sauna and solarium and golf may be played 1½ miles away. This part of Wessex is blessed with several places of historic appeal which may be reached within half-an-hour's drive and a fitting end to a day's excursions is to return with happy anticipation of a superb dinner served in the charming conservatory dining room with fine wines in attendance.

Please mention
Recommended COUNTRY HOTELS
when seeking refreshment or
accommodation at a Hotel
mentioned in these pages

Worcestershire

COLLIN HOUSE HOTEL,
Collin Lane, Broadway,
Worcestershire

Tel: 0386 858354*

Residential and restaurant licence; 7 bedrooms, 6 with private bathrooms; Historic interest; Children welcome; Car park (35); Oxford 36 miles, Evesham 6.

Tourists from all over the world flock to picturesque Broadway where, epitomising its old-world charm, the friendly little sixteenth century stone house is warmly recommended. It is of great character with mullioned windows, solid oak beams and inglenook fireplaces where logs crackle in cool weather. The hotel is located in a secluded situation one mile from Broadway village. Proprietors John and Judith Mills have skilfully maintained the original style whilst satisfying the most exacting modern requirements. Bedrooms are individually decorated to a high standard, two have four-poster beds and most have private bathrooms. Traditional English fare is served by candlelight in a beamed restaurant and there are two comfortable lounges in which to relax. A small open-air swimming pool is located in the pleasant grounds of eight acres.

GRAFTON MANOR COUNTRY HOUSE HOTEL,
Grafton Lane, Bromsgrove,
Worcestershire B61 7HA

Tel: 0527 31525/37247

Hotel licence; 9 bedrooms, all with private bathrooms; Historic interest; Car park (50); Kidderminster 10 miles.

Built by the Earl of Shrewsbury in 1567 on the site of a pre-Norman building, Grafton Manor was rebuilt in the early 18th century and still retains the style and elegance of that period. The Manor stands in 6 acres of well-tended gardens which incorporate a lake and herb garden. Within its mellow walls, modern-day guests will find their every requirement anticipated. Tastefully restored bedrooms are luxuriously furnished with real effect coal gas fires and each has a bathroom en suite, colour television, telephone, clock radio and various other thoughtful extras. Under the personal supervision of Chef/Proprietor John Morris, the cuisine matches the excellence of the comforts provided, much of the produce coming from the home estate.

THORNBURY HOUSE HOTEL,
Avenue Road, Great Malvern, Worcestershire WR14 3AR

Tel: 0684-52278

Residential licence; 19 bedrooms, some with en suite facilities; Children welcome; Car park; Worcester 7, Hereford 16 miles.

This delightful country house hotel stands in a quiet tree-lined avenue with a large south-facing garden; perfect for relaxation. All 19 bedrooms have colour television, washbasins, shaver points, and tea/coffee making facilities. Some are en suite, two would appeal to the more romantic, with four-poster beds. The hotel is situated only three minutes' walk from Great Malvern station, yet is close to the Winter Gardens and Town Centre. There is ample car parking. Thornbury House Hotel is well placed for touring the surrounding area where you can enjoy, amongst other events, Gala Days, and the Malvern Festival. The restaurant offers a comprehensive à la carte menu from 6 p.m. to 10 p.m. each evening. American Express, Access, Diners and Visa cards all accepted. Full details on request from Carol and John Knight. *AA**, RAC**.*

THE OLD VICARAGE,
Hanley Road, Malvern Wells, Worcestershire WR14 4PH

Tel: 06845-2585 or 0684-572585

Restaurant and residential licence; 6 bedrooms, all with private bathrooms; Children and dogs welcome; Car park (8); Hereford 20 miles.

The Old Vicarage is a house of striking character, set in its own spacious lawned gardens on the slopes of the Malvern Hills. Guest rooms are large double or twin rooms, elegantly furnished and all with full en suite facilities and colour television. Interesting and varied menus (all home prepared) are offered in our licensed diningroom. The Old Vicarage provides easy access to the Cotswolds and Malvern Hills. *ETB* 🌷 🌷 🌷

HOLDFAST COTTAGE HOTEL,
Welland, Near Malvern, Worcestershire WR13 6NA

Tel: 0684 310288

Residential and restaurant licence; 9 bedrooms, 8 with private bathrooms; Historic interest; Children and dogs welcome; Car park (16); Tewkesbury 13 miles.

Built in the seventeenth century as a farmhouse but much enlarged in Victorian times, this delightful little country retreat lies in the lee of the Malvern Hills in two acres of lovely gardens. With its oak beams giving evidence of its antiquity, this is a recommended hotel noted for its friendly atmosphere, personal service and excellent food and wine. Public and private rooms are delightfully decorated and there are many antique furnishings and log fires to augment the central heating to complete the feeling of warmth and well-being. Most guest rooms have a private bath or shower and there is a comfortable lounge and bar.

North Yorkshire

SHIP INN,
Acaster Malbis, York,
Yorkshire (North)

Tel: 0904 705609 and 703888

Licensed; 5 bedrooms; Historic interest; Children welcome; Car park (30); Leeds 17 miles, York 3½.

A really picturesque holiday retreat on the banks of the Yorkshire Ouse, this attractive and well-run hostelry is yet only a short distance from the magnificence of York, the United Kingdom's second most popular tourist attraction. Offering first-class fare and spruce accommodation, the inn makes a superb holiday headquarters and is equally popular with boating enthusiasts and businessmen. Excellent evening dinners are served in the relaxed olde-worlde atmosphere of the Wheelhouse Restaurant, whilst a wide range of lunches and evening snacks may be enjoyed in the friendly Riverside Bar adjacent to which is a garden where children may disport themselves in summer. Those with a penchant for fishing may be well accommodated and the inn has its own moorings for residents and visitors. Further afield, the Yorkshire Dales beckon and the coast may be reached in less than an hour.

WHITFIELD HOUSE HOTEL,
Darnholm, Goathland,
Yorkshire (North) YO22 5LA

Tel: 0947 86215

Restaurant and residential licence; 10 bedrooms, 5 with private bathrooms; Children over 3 welcome, dogs by arrangement; Car park (10), garages (2); Whitby 9 miles.

Located in the heart of the beautiful North York Moors National Park, the Whitfield House Hotel is a warm and welcoming base from which to explore many lovely dales and to visit the host of ancient abbeys, castles and stately homes in the area or the well-known resorts of the Yorkshire coast. Comfortable accommodation is augmented by delicious and ample home cooking. *AA*; Guestaccom; Les Routiers Approved; ETB* 👑 👑 👑.

FOXHOLM HOTEL,
Ebberston, Near Scarborough,
Yorkshire (North)

Tel: 0723 85550*

Residential licence; 10 bedrooms, 1 with private bathroom, 5 with showers; Children and dogs welcome; Car park (12); York 30 miles, Scarborough 10, Pickering 7.

Part of a delightful old-world village scene, Foxholm is a farmhouse converted into a small comfortable licensed country hotel offering full central heating, colour television in the lounge and radio in the bedrooms. There are fine views across a large enclosed garden and good home cooking with a choice of menu and home-grown vegetables is to be enjoyed. Kay and Andy Clyde give personal attention in this family-run hotel which is an ideal centre for touring moors, dales and coast, with York and Scarborough within easy reach. Open from March to November and at Christmas, terms for dinner, bed and breakfast are from £21.00 with weekly reductions. A brochure is available on request. *ETB* 🌷 🌷 🌷*; AA, RAC recommended; Les Routiers.*

SIMONSTONE HALL,
Hawes,
Yorkshire (North) DL8 3LY

Tel: 09697 255

Licensed; 10 bedrooms, all with private bathrooms; Dogs welcome; Car park (24); London 250 miles, Kendal 26, Kirkby Lonsdale 23, Settle 22, Leyburn 16.

Situated on the Buttertubs Pass, just one-and-a-half miles from the market town of Hawes, Simonstone Hall is a delightful 250-year-old building enjoying unsurpassed southerly views across Wensleydale. Its large rooms are comfortably furnished with antiques giving the aura and grace of a bygone age but with the essential luxuries of the twentieth century. These include central heating, excellent cuisine, extensive wine list, unique Tawny Owl bar, and all bedrooms with colour television and tea/coffee makers. The hotel is open all year round and offers autumn to spring breaks, as well as Christmas and New Year house parties. Dogs are made welcome at all times and Simonstone Hall is under the personal management of the resident owners, Mr and Mrs B. Jeffryes and their family.

THE MOORLANDS HOTEL,
Levisham, Pickering,
Yorkshire (North) YO18 7NL
Tel: 0751 60229

Residential licence; 5 bedrooms, all with private bathrooms; Car park (10); York 26 miles, Scarborough 17.

Guests are assured of a warm Yorkshire welcome at this family run hotel. Located in the unspoilt village of Levisham it is ideally situated in the North York Moors National Park, within easy reach of the coast and the historic town of York. Good home cooking using fresh produce, mostly home grown. The Moorlands has for some years been a "No smoking" hotel and this has proved very popular with guests who wish to enjoy their stay in a pleasant atmosphere. Evening Dinner, Bed and Breakfast from £20; Bed and Breakfast from £14.

RIVERDALE COUNTRY HOUSE HOTEL,
Bainbridge, Leyburn,
Yorkshire (North) DL8 3EW
Tel: 0969-50311/09693-381

(November-March)

Restaurant and residential licence; 14 bedrooms, 11 with private bathrooms; Car park; Skipton 31 miles, Leyburn 12, Hawes 4.

Situated in the centre of an attractive Wensleydale village overlooking the green and stocks, Riverdale House is a warm, welcoming base for those interested in touring or walking the famous Yorkshire Dales-James Herriot country. The hotel is personally run by the owner Mrs M. Harrison and offers all the comforts expected by guests nowadays — private bathroom, colour television, hot drinks facilities and central heating. The restaurant is renowned for excellent home made food cooked with finest fresh ingredients. Bargain Breaks March and November. *ETB* 🏵️🏵️.

COTTAGE LEAS COUNTRY HOTEL,
Middleton, Near Pickering,
Yorkshire (North) YO18 8PN
Tel: 0751 72129

Restaurant and residential licence; 16 bedrooms, all with private bathrooms; Historic interest; Children and dogs welcome; Car park (50); Pickering 2 miles.

Cottage Leas is an elegant country farmhouse hotel retaining many of its original 17th century features and standing in its own impressive grounds, surrounded by open fields. The hotel enjoys picturesque views over the Vale of Pickering and is within easy reach of the market towns of Pickering and Kirbymoorside. Relax in the delightful farmhouse lounge with the beautiful open log fire ensuring a warm welcome. Our menu is varied and interesting, and is complemented by our wine list. All bedrooms are en suite and all have colour televisions. *ETB* 🏵️🏵️🏵️.

MONK FRYSTON HALL,
Monk Fryston, Leeds,
Yorkshire (North) LS25 5DU

Tel: 0977 682369

Licensed; 29 bedrooms, all with private bathrooms; Historic interest; Children and dogs welcome; Car park (60); Doncaster 19 miles, Leeds 14.

Serving holidaymakers and businessmen with equal facility, this lovely old manor house exudes the warmest of welcomes through its mullioned windows, rich oak-panelled lounges and bars, log fires and willing service. Peacefully ensconced in wooded grounds where a wide terrace leads to the Italian gardens and an ornamental lake, the hotel is an historic attraction in its own right but being only a short distance from the A1, is conveniently placed for the county's tourist and commercial centres. Guest rooms are beautifully appointed; all have a private bathroom, colour television, radio and direct-dial telephone. Just as excellent is the catering for which a deserved reputation has been achieved for the extensive choice of à la carte and table d'hôte dishes.

BLACKSMITHS ARMS HOTEL,
Rosedale Abbey, Pickering,
Yorkshire (North) YO18 8EN

Tel: 07-515 331

Licensed; 12 bedrooms, all with private bathrooms; Historic interest; Car park (80); Scarborough 14 miles.

The Blacksmiths Arms is situated at the southern end of Rosedale in the North Yorkshire Moors National Park, surrounded by outstanding beauty. The hotel has been tastefully extended to provide for the needs of the modern traveller, with full central heating and open log fires. It offers twelve bedrooms, all en suite, with colour television; tea/coffee making facilities, clock radio and views of the moors and forests. The restaurant is renowned for its excellent food and tasteful decor. An extensive table d'hôte menu is available every evening (changes daily). *AA**, RAC**, ETB* ♛ ♛ ♛ ♛.

THE LODGE COUNTRY HOUSE HOTEL,
Middleton Road, Pickering,
Yorkshire (North) YO18 8NQ

Tel: 0751 72976

Restaurant licence; 9 bedrooms, all with private facilities; Children welcome; Car park (12); York 26 miles, Scarborough 20.

Small it may be but as a base from which to explore the North York Moors National Park, The Lodge offers excellent accommodation at reasonable rates in three family suites, three double and three twin-bedded rooms, all of which have en suite bathrooms or shower rooms, central heating and tea and coffee-making facilities. Every modern comfort is here to aid relaxation from open fires and spacious, comfortable lounges (one with colour television) to the worthy traditional English cuisine. Situated in its own extensive grounds of mature trees, lawns and shrubberies, this little jewel of an establishment will appeal to both tourist and sportsman for there are opportunities for fishing, golf, riding and swimming nearby.

HACKNESS GRANGE COUNTRY HOTEL,
Near Scarborough,
Yorkshire (North) YO13 0JW

Tel: 0723 82345

Licensed; 27 bedrooms, all with private bathrooms; Children welcome; Car park; York 41 miles, Whitby 20.

Within the splendours of the North York Moors National Park, this fine hotel is yet only a short distance from the popular family resort of Scarborough. The River Derwent flows round the 11 acres of grounds which enclose a trout pool, tennis court and pitch and putt, whilst forest trails and mountain walks stretch in all directions. Riding and trekking may be arranged and there is an indoor swimming pool. Guest rooms are delightfully furnished and all have en suite facilities, direct-dial telephone, mini-bars, radio and child listening devices. The cuisine is excellent and features home garden produce. Terms for accommodation at this delightful place are far from excessive.

STONE HOUSE HOTEL,
Sedbusk, Near Hawes,
Yorkshire (North) DL8 3PT

Tel: 096-97 571*

Residential and restaurant licence; 15 bedrooms, 14 with private bathrooms; Historic interest; Children and dogs welcome; Car park (15); Ripon 36 miles, Kendal 26.

In the heart of the Yorkshire Dales National Park, this fine house was built in the reign of King Edward VII, an era of opulence and elegance that is reflected today as the house performs sterling duty as a country house hotel. Secluded in a lovely Old English garden with views of the foothills of the Pennines from its windows, Stone House serves guests of active or passive disposition equally well. A cosy bar, library and billiard room provide unexacting recreation whilst, as a change from fell walking, lawn tennis may be played in the grounds. The majority of the guest rooms have private facilities and wholesome, home-cooked Yorkshire food will satisfy the most hearty appetite.

GRASSINGTON HOUSE HOTEL,
Grassington, Skipton-in-Craven,
Yorkshire (North) BD23 5AQ

Tel: 0756 752406*

Restaurant and residential licence; 19 bedrooms, 7 with private bathrooms; Historic interest; Children and dogs welcome; Car park (20); Ripon 22 miles.

This creeper-clad stone house overlooks the cobbled village square and, as a friendly touring centre for the Yorkshire Dales National Park, is hard to beat for comfort and value. A Grade II listed building, the house has tastefully decorated bedrooms, some of which have private facilities. The lounge, with colour television, is made for quiet relaxation and at the rear of the hotel is a bungalow annexe, ideal for those who find stairs a problem. Dinner is served at 7 p.m. Bar meals are available from noon to 2 p.m. and packed lunches may be ordered in advance. There is good fishing in the River Wharfe and golf at Skipton.

THE WENSLEYDALE HEIFER,
West Witton, Near Leyburn,
Yorkshire (North) DL8 4LS

Tel: 0969 22322

Licensed; 20 bedrooms, all with private bathrooms; Historic interest; Children and dogs welcome; Car park (30); Leyburn 4 miles.

A most characterful seventeenth century hotel with a lovely walled garden set in the heart of Wensleydale, James Herriot country. The addition of modern comforts such as central heating and private facilities in all of the bedrooms has by no means diminished the hotel's original character and the old oak beams, roaring log fires and antique furniture — including four poster beds in some of the rooms — are a delight to behold. With a fast growing reputation for its fine table and excellent cellar the Wensleydale Heifer is a perfect rendezvous for meeting friends for a meal or a drink — or for spoiling yourself for a long weekend!

WHITWELL HALL COUNTRY HOUSE HOTEL,
Whitwell-on-the-Hill, York,
Yorkshire (North)

Tel: 065-381 551

Residential and restaurant licence; 12 bedrooms, all with private bathrooms; coach house 8 bedrooms, all with private bathrooms; Car park (40), garages (4); York 12 miles, Malton 6.

Built in Tudor gothic style, this gracious country house provides first-class accommodation and a rare opportunity for guests to enjoy very good English food. It enjoys superb views towards York and there is much of historic interest in the area, including York, Castle Howard and Herriot country. The house itself has numerous interesting architectural features; a fine cantilevered staircase leads to a balcony and charmingly appointed guest rooms, all of which have their own bath/shower facilities, colour televisions, direct dial telephones and radios and overlook the beautiful gardens. Meals are served in an elegant diningroom and there is a separate conference room, with more bedrooms in the Coach House block which has recently been modernised and refurnished and is ideal for small, important prestige meetings. Guests over 18 years only. The grounds extend to 18 acres, featuring terraced lawns, woodland walks and a hard tennis court and the hotel has an indoor heated swimming pool and sauna and a games room. *AA***, RAC***, Egon Ronay. ETB* 👑 👑 👑 👑.

LASTINGHAM GRANGE COUNTRY HOUSE HOTEL,
Lastingham, York,
Yorkshire (North) YO6 6TH

Tel: 075-15 345*

Restaurant and residential licence; 12 bedrooms, all with private bathrooms; Children and dogs welcome; Car park; Leeds 24 miles.

Transformed from a 17th century farmhouse, the lovely old stone-built grange stands in 10 acres of gardens and fields with scenic grandeur on all sides. Apart from its highly regarded cuisine and service, the hotel has excellent accommodation, guest rooms being furnished in individual style and incorporating a private bathroom, radio and baby-listening device in each; the views from the windows are magnificent. Central heating is backed up by a cheerful log fire in the spacious lounge in cool weather. There is much of historic and geographic interest in the North York Moors National Park; one may fish, ride or play golf in the vicinity and the coast is only 20 miles away.

West Yorkshire

THE HEY GREEN HOTEL,
Marsden, Near Huddersfield,
Yorkshire (West) HD7 6NJ

Tel: 0484 844235

Licensed; 10 bedrooms, all with private bathrooms; Historic interest; Children welcome; Car park (80); Huddersfield 7 miles.

The Hey Green is a former country house, originally built in 1786 for the Crowthers of Bankdam, and stands in eight acres of its own picturesque grounds in this lovely and unspoilt corner of Yorkshire. Recently subject to an extensive modernisation programme, it yet retains the charms of its origins. The 10 bedrooms have private facilities, as well as colour television with video channel, telephone, radio, hot drinks facilities, and a fully stocked drinks refrigerator. Delicious table d'hôte and à la carte is offered in the restaurant, while bar meals are available in the public bar for those with a lighter appetite. Short breaks are available all year round. *AA***, RAC***.*

Other specialised

FHG PUBLICATIONS

* Recommended SHORT-BREAK HOLIDAYS IN BRITAIN   £2.95

* Recommended WAYSIDE INNS OF BRITAIN   £2.95

* PETS WELCOME!   £1.95

* BED AND BREAKFAST IN BRITAIN   £1.95

Published annually. Please add 30p postage (U.K. only) when ordering from the publishers:

FHG PUBLICATIONS LTD
Abbey Mill Business Centre, Seedhill,
Paisley, Renfrewshire PA1 1JN

Dyfed

BEGGARS REACH HOTEL,
Burton, Near Milford Haven,
Dyfed

Tel: 0646 600700 and 600560*

Licensed; 10 bedrooms, all with private bathrooms; Children and dogs welcome; Car park (36); Haverfordwest 9 miles.

This peaceful country house hotel was once an early Victorian rectory and is situated close to the Cleddau Estuary. Considerable modernisation has provided excellent guest rooms, some of family size, all with bathrooms en suite. Set in a very quiet position it is an ideal base for exploring Pembrokeshire. Please write or telephone for brochure and tariff.

Taking a pet on holiday? Then buy
"PETS WELCOME!"

THE ANIMAL LOVERS' HOLIDAY GUIDE
Details of Hotels, Guest Houses, Furnished Accommodation, Caravans, etc. where holiday makers and their pets are made welcome.
*Available from most newsagents and bookshops price £1.95
or from Publishers (please add 30p postage)*
**FHG PUBLICATIONS LTD
Abbey Mill Business Centre, Seedhill,
Paisley, Renfrewshire PA1 1JN**

CASTELL MALGWYN HOTEL,
Llechryd, Cardigan,
Dyfed SA43 2QA

Tel: 023-987 382

Licensed; 23 bedrooms, all with private bathrooms; Children welcome; Car park; Carmarthen 27 miles, Cardigan 3.

An elegant country mansion, Castell Malgwyn matches the aura of its historic past with skilfully blended modern refinements. The creeper-clad house is set in a 42 acre estate with many mature trees and woodland walks. The grounds also incorporate a putting green and a swimming pool which is heated in the summer. Much thought and imagination has gone into the planning of these services. Guest rooms are a delight with their attractive furnishings and the luxury appointments include colour television, tea and coffee making and en suite facilities. The cuisine at this lovely country house is excellent with an extensive choice offered from both the table d'hôte and the à la carte menus. Local produce is offered whenever possible and a well stocked wine cellar complements the appetising dishes. Apart from the pleasures of the countryside with its variety of sports including golf courses and pony trekking, holiday-makers will find the beaches of Cardigan Bay nearby. *AA, RAC***.*

TREGYNON COUNTRY FARM HOTEL,
Gwaun Valley, Near Fishguard,
Dyfed SA65 9TU

Tel: 0239 820531

Restaurant and residential licence; 6 bedrooms, 3 with private bathrooms; Historic interest; Children welcome; Car park; London 263 miles, Carmarthen 45, Cardigan 19.

In the Pembrokeshire Coast National Park with superb views over the Gwaun Valley, this beamed sixteenth century award-winning farmhouse offers a country house holiday where lovers of good food will feel at home. Renowned for its traditional cuisine with wholefood and vegetarian specialities, as featured in 'Here's Health', Tregynon uses fresh produce from the farm wherever possible, including its own trout. Virtually everything is made on the premises, including the oak-smoking of gammon and bacon using traditional methods, while sausages, breads, rolls and organic cheeses are made without additives. Accommodation is comfortable and public rooms warm and cosy with log fires in winter. The grounds boast an iron-age fort, 200 ft. waterfall, forest and wildlife. Two-day 'Great Little Breaks' at special rates from October to March. *WTB ❀ ❀ ❀. RAC 'Acclaimed'.*

STONE HALL,
Welsh Hook, Haverfordwest, Dyfed SA62 5NS

Tel: 0348 840212

Restaurant and residential licence; 6 bedrooms, all with private bathrooms; Historic interest; Children welcome; Car park (50); Carmarthen 28 miles.

Conveniently situated six miles from both the West and North coasts of Pembrokeshire with its unspoilt sandy beaches and coves below the rugged cliffs. The hotel is in a secluded, tranquil location in ten acres of gardens and woodland and was recently converted from a fourteenth century manor house extended in early Georgian and Victorian times. The styles of each period have been carefully preserved. The cosy bar and restaurant are in the oldest part and have slate-flagged floors, the original oak beams and an inglenook fireplace with a log fire most of the year. Genuine French cuisine prepared from fresh produce is served in the restaurant and is recommended by Egon Ronay. À la carte and table d'hôte menus are provided. *WTB* ❀ ❀ ❀.

COURT HOTEL,
Lamphey, Pembroke, Dyfed SA71 5NT

Tel: 0646 672273

Licensed; 21 bedrooms and 8 flats, all with private bathrooms; Historic interest; Children welcome; Car park; Tenby 10 miles, Pembroke 2.

Woods, ponds and a trout stream feature in the tranquil grounds which surround this welcoming Georgian country house. Guests are assured of friendly and efficient service, especially in the attractive Georgian Restaurant where one may dine by candlelight from an extensive à la carte menu. Guest rooms are spacious and luxuriously appointed with bathroom en suite, colour television and telephone as standard. Some family rooms are available in which children sharing are accepted free. A recent innovation is a superb leisure complex with a heated indoor pool with toddlers' area, sauna, solarium and mini-gym. The Pembrokeshire coast is near at hand and opportunities exist for a variety of outdoor pursuits.

BIKEREHYD FARM,
Pennant, Llanon, Dyfed SY23 5PB

Tel: 09746 365

Restaurant licence; 6 bedrooms, 4 with private bathrooms; Historic interest; Children and dogs welcome; Car park (8); Aberystwyth 12 miles.

Bikerehyd Farm is part of the remains of a 14th century village. In the warm and comfortable farmhouse there are three charming bedrooms, two with double beds and one with twin beds. These rooms can combine to make an en suite family room. Tea and coffee making facilities are available to guests. The lounge has a colour television and open fire. The farm is ideally situated to enable the visitor to see many places of scenic and historic interest. *AA Listed, WTB Award.*

WARPOOL COURT HOTEL,
St. David's,
Dyfed SA62 6BN
Tel: 0437 720300*

Licensed; 25 bedrooms, all with private bathrooms; Historic interest; Children and dogs welcome; Car park (100); Haverfordwest 12 miles.

Renowned for its warmth of welcome, food, service and accommodation, this well-furnished hotel, situated within walking distance of St. David's Cathedral, overlooks the wild Atlantic on a remote peninsula of rugged beauty which is steeped in history and famous for its variety of bird life and flora. The facilities here provide memorable family holidays in delightful surroundings. The hotel is imaginatively furnished and is known for its equally imaginative cuisine. Salmon and mackerel are smoked on the premises and finest use is made of locally grown produce. Meals are served in a spacious restaurant with glorious views over St. Brides Bay. The residents' lounge overlooks the Italian gardens and sea and there is a covered heating swimming pool, tennis court, sauna, gymnasium and games room.

WHITESANDS BAY HOTEL,
St. David's,
Dyfed SA62 6PT
Tel: 0437 720403

Licensed; 5 suites, 14 double and 2 single bedrooms, 12 with private bathrooms; Children and dogs welcome — by arrangement; Car park (100); Haverfordwest 17 miles, Fishguard 16.

Peace, luxury, magnificent views and some of the best bathing and surfing in Britain are attractions that lure discriminating holidaymakers to this fine Three Star Hotel. The facilities offered here are really something special with thoughtful amenities and diversions for guests of all ages, to say nothing of the superb accommodation, all bedrooms having colour television, radio and baby-listening devices. Appetites sharpened by the fresh, clean air are well satisfied by first-class food and wines and the Tall Ships Bar is a convivial meeting place. Paddling pool, games room and swings are popular and there is a super outdoor pool, sauna and solarium. *ETB* ❀ ❀ ❀.

WAUNGRON FARM HOTEL,
Whitland,
Dyfed SA34 0QX
Tel: 0994 240682*

Licensed; 14 bedrooms, all with private bathrooms; Children welcome, dogs by arrangement; Car park (100); Haverfordwest 16 miles, Carmarthen 14.

Comfortable accommodation on ground level in rural setting. Ideally placed for touring the Preseli Hills and the villages and sandy beaches of the Pembrokeshire Coast National Park. The accommodation is somewhat out of the ordinary with cowsheds skilfully converted into award-winning guest rooms, all of which have private bath or shower, colour television, radio and tea/coffee facilities. A bridal suite has a four poster bed and the executive suite has a jacuzzi bath. Excellent table d'hôte and à la carte meals are served in the Barn Restaurant or farmhouse diningroom, using fresh local produce.

Glamorgan

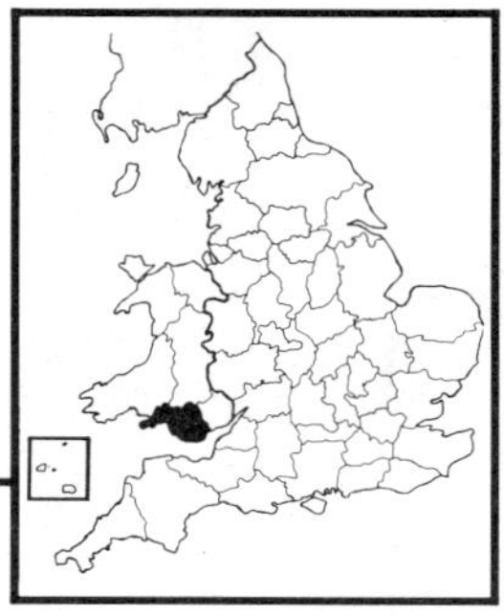

MISKIN MANOR,
Miskin,
Mid-Glamorgan CF7 8ND

Tel: 0443 224204

Licensed; 32 bedrooms, all with private bathrooms; Historic interest; Children welcome; Car park (100); Llantrisant 2 miles.

Occupying the site of the original manor (circa 1092), this lovely mid-Victorian building has many virtues. With mullioned windows gazing out over the River Ely and 22 acres of garden and woodland, the house has recently been refurbished to exacting modern standards and now provides luxurious comfort in beautifully furnished public and private rooms. Each spacious guest room is individual in style and decor and appointed with its own bathroom, colour television, radio, direct-dial telephone and many more thoughtful touches. Attention to detail and willing service lists this establishment well above the average. Most rooms have superb views and some have four-posters. There is even a suite where the future King Edward VIII stayed in the 1920's. A wide ranging à la carte luncheon and dinner menu is presented in a magnificently panelled restaurant. The cuisine is traditionally British at its most splendid and there is a most interesting selection of wines. Adjacent to the hotel is Frederick's, a delightfully equipped, modern leisure centre where the facilities cater for all ages and tastes. These include squash, swimming and badminton whilst there is also a fine gymnasium, solarium, sauna, snooker room, spa, bistro and bar. The hotel caters for conferences, promotional and private functions in a big way and such amenities are unsurpassed.

PLEASE ENCLOSE A STAMPED ADDRESSED ENVELOPE WHEN WRITING TO ENQUIRE ABOUT ACCOMMODATION FEATURED IN THIS GUIDE

Gwent

LLANWENARTH HOUSE,
Govilon, Abergavenny,
Gwent NP7 9SF

Tel: 0873 830289*

Restaurant and residential licence; 5 bedrooms, all with private shower/bathrooms; Historic interest; Children over 5 years and dogs welcome; Car park (7), garages (2); London 150 miles, Cardiff 32.

Dating from the sixteenth century, this lovely old manor house is set in peaceful and beautiful grounds within the Brecon Beacons National Park. The subject of painstaking renovation and restoration, the house offers the highest standards of comfort and cuisine. Guests are personally looked after by Bruce and Amanda Weatherill and their family. Amanda is a Cordon Bleu cook. Dinner is served by candlelight and private parties are catered for. Guest rooms enjoy lovely views; all are spacious and have private bath facilities. Central heating is installed throughout. Sporting opportunities abound in the area. *ETB* 👑 👑 👑 👑

Please mention
Recommended COUNTRY HOTELS
when seeking refreshment or
accommodation at a Hotel
mentioned in these pages

Gwynedd

TREFEDDIAN HOTEL,
Aberdovey,
Gwynedd LL35 0SB   Tel: 065-472 213*

Licensed; 46 bedrooms, all with private bathrooms; Children and dogs welcome; Car park (40), garage (20); Aberystwyth 29 miles.

The Trefeddian Hotel is a family owned and run hotel with a magnificent view overlooking golf links, sandy beach and Cardigan Bay. Facilities include an indoor heated swimming pool, badminton court, table tennis and games room. A hard tennis court is also available, and a nine-hole pitch and putt course. Water sports facilities are available on the estuary of the River Dovey. The bedrooms are well equipped, with colour television, radio, baby listening service, telephone and central heating. The hotel is an ideal centre for touring the Snowdonia National Park and for visiting the RSPB bird reserve, and the Tal-y-Llyn narrow gauge railway. *WTB* ❀ ❀ ❀ ❀; *AA, RAC***; Egon Ronay recommended.*

PARCIAU MAWR HOTEL,
Criccieth,
Gwynedd LL52 0RP   Tel: 076-671 2368*

Residential and restaurant licence; 13 bedrooms, 9 with private bathrooms; Children and dogs welcome; Car park; Caernarfon 15 miles.

Small, bright, comfortable and tastefully furnished, Parciau Mawr Hotel offers first-rate country house facilities by the sea. Approached by a driveway direct from the village High Street, the house stands secluded in grounds of 3½ acres yet is near all the attractions and sandy beaches of the little resort. Snowdonia with its attendant pleasures lies immediately inland. Beautifully decorated throughout, the hotel has superb bedrooms, all of which are centrally heated and have colour television installed. An annexe houses six rooms, all of which have private showers as well. A spacious lounge, sun lounge and bar each contribute their appeal whilst the excellent and varied cuisine, served in a delightful restaurant, will ensure happy memories of a sojourn here.

HENLLYS HALL HOTEL,
Beaumaris, Anglesey
Gwynedd LL58 8HU

Tel: 0248 810412
Fax: 0248 811511

Licensed; 25 bedrooms, all with private bathrooms; Historical interest; Children and dogs welcome; Car park (100); London 246 miles, Holyhead 25, Caernarfon 12.

Steeped in history, Henllys Hall was originally the home of the Welsh Princes of Gwynedd. Now an hotel of immense character, this grand establishment stands majestically in 40 acres of grounds overlooking the Menai Straits. Apart from superb cuisine and luxurious accommodation, guests are offered a variety of first class leisure amenities and there is a tennis court, heated outdoor swimming pool, health complex, table tennis, pool table, cellar restaurant and bar, and several function rooms. Children are welcome, and there is a laundry and baby-listening service. This is a romantic place for an off-season weekend break and several four poster rooms are available.

BRYN CREGIN GARDEN HOTEL,
Ty Mawr Road, Deganwy, Near Conwy,
Gwynedd LL31 9UR

Tel: 0492 85266/83402

Restaurant and residential licence; 16 bedrooms, all with private bathrooms; Children welcome; Car park (30); Llandudno 2 miles.

The Bryn Cregin Garden Hotel was built in the 1890's as a private home for a retired ship's captain and was converted to an hotel in the 1930's. Set in its own magnificent gardens the hotel enjoys spectacular views over the Conwy Estuary, Conwy Castle and the Snowdonia hills beyond. It is perfectly situated for guests to enjoy golfing, sailing, walking and sightseeing. The bedrooms are individually furnished and most overlook the Estuary and garden. Every room has colour television, direct dial telephone, clock/radio and tea/coffee making facilities. Suites and four-poster beds are available on request. Our restaurant is featured in many good food guides and is British Tourist Authority Commended. We enjoy a fine reputation locally and pride ourselves on serving only the freshest, best quality food.

PALÉ HALL,
Llandderfel, Near Bala,
Gwynedd

Tel: 067-83 285

Licensed; 17 bedrooms, all with private bathrooms; Historic interest; Children welcome; Car park (150); London 211 miles, Betws-y-Coed 22, Dolgellau 18.

Modern-day guests will find this imposing nineteenth century mansion just as enchanting as did Queen Victoria. Lovingly restored and unashamedly opulent in its role as a regal country hotel, Palé Hall incorporates contemporary refinements that blend unobtrusively into the mellow atmosphere. Each bedroom has a luxurious bathroom en suite, colour television and direct-dial telephone and two also have their own jacuzzi. Superb public rooms include a lounge with magnificent hand painted dome ceiling, and a bar made up from marble fireplaces is a delightful place for an aperitif before coming to terms with the faultless cuisine.

TIR-Y-COED COUNTRY HOUSE HOTEL,
Rowen, Conwy,
Gwynedd LL32 8TP

Tel: 0492 650219*

Restaurant and residential licence; 8 bedrooms, all with private bathrooms/showers; Children and dogs welcome; Car park (8); Colwyn Bay 10 miles, Conwy 4.

Only three miles from the famous Bodnant Gardens, this comfortable little hotel has enchanting landscaped grounds of its own. Within easy reach of the Conwy Valley, Snowdonia and the sandy baches of Anglesey, the hotel has well-appointed guest rooms, all of which have a private bath or shower and tea and coffee-making trays; most have superb views and all rooms have their own colour television. Public rooms include an attractive lounge and pleasant cocktail bar, whilst dishes, traditionally cooked and personally prepared by Resident Proprietors, Ken and Gwyneth Kirkham, are served in a delightful dining room.

TYNYCORNEL HOTEL,
Talyllyn, Tywyn,
Gwynedd LL36 9AJ

Tel: 065-477 282

Licensed; 16 bedrooms, most with private bathrooms; Historic interest; Children and dogs welcome; Car park; Aberystwyth 26 miles, Machynlleth 10.

A jewel set amidst magnificent mountain scenery, this fine hotel can claim to cater for all tastes and inclinations. Sailing, wind-surfing and canoeing may be enjoyed on the hotel's own lake during the summer and it is only a short distance to the famous Talyllyn Narrow Gauge Railway which runs down the valley to the coast. However, it is the fisherman who is probably best served for the lake is noted for its excellent trout fishing and rights are free of charge to residents. Well-appointed accommodation is available in the main building and two adjacent annexes and dining by candlelight is a memorable experience. The hotel has a sauna and solarium and an outdoor heated swimming pool.

Powys

OLD GWERNYFED COUNTRY MANOR,
Three Cocks, Brecon,
Powys

Tel: 049-74 376*

Residential and restaurant licence; 11 bedrooms, 9 with private bathrooms; Historic interest; Children and dogs welcome; Car park; Hereford 25 miles, Abergavenny 18, Builth Wells 9.

A splendid Elizabethan manor house set in its own grounds of four acres in the foothills of the Black Mountains, Old Gwernyfed is a truly delightful retreat with many notable architectural features. These include a minstrels' gallery overlooking the oak-panelled banqueting hall, the cunningly concealed 'Escape Hatch', Priests' Hole and Spanish Armada Mast. Dining by candlelight in this tranquil place is a memorable experience with home-cooked dishes presenting several delicious specialities. Guest rooms are full of character and have superb views of the mountains or Wye Valley. With many sporting activities available in the area, this is a recommended place in which to recover life's values. Evenings may be spent chatting in the bar, playing table tennis and croquet or even trying the grand piano for sound.

YNYSHIR HALL COUNTRY HOUSE HOTEL,
Eglwysfach, Machynlleth,
Powys SY20 8TA

Tel: 065-474 209*

Residential licence; 9 bedrooms, 8 with private bathrooms; Historic interest; Children and dogs welcome; Car park (10); Aberystwyth 12 miles.

Fondly remembered for its friendliness, good service and high standard of modern amenities, the elegant, sixteenth century Ynyshir Hall nestles in 10 acres of garden and woodland alongside the River Dovey and surrounded by the Ynyshir Bird Reserve. Log fires contribute to an atmosphere in which relaxation comes easily, public rooms and bedrooms being furnished in sumptuous comfort: there is one guest room on the ground floor, ideal for those unable to manage the stairs. Fresh fruit and vegetables form the hotel's walled kitchen garden feature on the interesting menu presented in a well-planned and attractive dining room.

LAKE HOTEL,
Llangammarch Wells,
Powys LD4 4BS

Tel: 059-12 202

Residential and restaurant licence; 19 bedrooms, all with private bathrooms; Dogs welcome; Brecon 31 miles, Llandovery 14, Llanwrtyd Wells 4.

Over the years, visitors from all over the world have come to this well recommended hotel, many of them to sample the waters from the rare barium spring in the grounds. No less are the attractions of the first rate cuisine and accommodation, qualities backed by a caring and courteous staff. Residents are encouraged to make full use of the many sporting activities available in the delightful 50-acres of secluded grounds. These include a 9-hole golf course and putting green and a lake. The hotel also has rights for over five and a half miles of salmon and trout fishing. Clay pigeon shoots are held regularly and hacking ponies are available.

LLWYNDERW HOTEL,
Abergwesyn, Llanwrtyd Wells,
Powys LD5 4TW

Tel: 059-13 238*

Residential and restaurant licence; 10 bedrooms, 2 suites, all with private bathrooms; Historic interest; Children over 10 welcome, dogs by arrangement; Car park; Brecon 27 miles, Llandovery 10.

With magnificent views of the surrounding mountains and countryside, this fine Georgian house dates from 1796 and stands 1000 feet above sea level in a wild and beautiful part of Mid-Wales. Tranquillity, comfort and elegance are the hallmarks of the hotel and all of the guest rooms are individually decorated, mostly with antique furniture. Cooking in traditional style presents a memorable six-course dinner menu and an extensive wine list complements the meal. This house is ideal for a relaxing holiday and terms represent excellent value.

LLUGWY HALL COUNTRY HOUSE HOTEL,
Pennal, Machynlleth,
Powys SY20 9JX

Tel: 065-475 228/622

Licensed; 11 bedrooms, 9 with private bathrooms; Historic interest; Children and dogs welcome; Car park (40); Aberystwyth 18 miles.

For a really refreshing holiday on one of the most beautiful estates in Wales, Llugwy Hall offers peace and comfort as well as excellent food and service. Individually furnished guest rooms are exquisitely appointed and enjoy delightful views of the Merioneth mountains. In the 40-acre grounds there are opportunities for self-catering in lodges, cottages, apartments and flatlets. The lawns stretch down to the banks of the River Dovey on which one may fish for salmon and trout. Children are very welcome and well catered for. A variety of indoor and outdoor games will appeal to guests of all ages.

Aberdeenshire

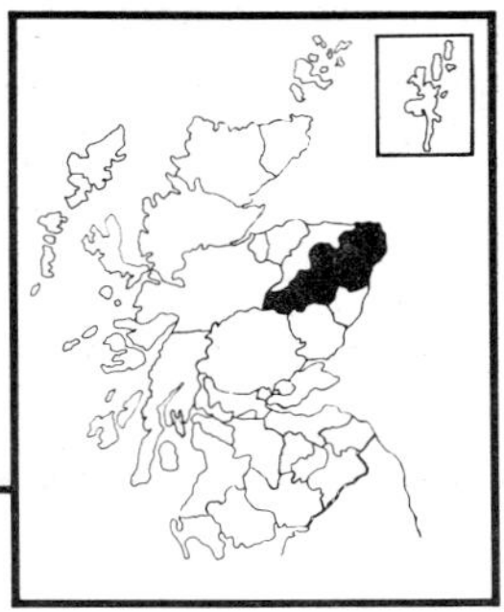

CASTLE HOTEL,
Huntly,
Aberdeenshire   Tel: 0466 2696*

Licensed; 20 double bedrooms, 4 single, 10 with private bathrooms; Historic interest; Children and dogs welcome; Car park; Aberdeen 39 miles, Banff 21.

Built in 1750 as a Dower House for the Duchess of Gordon, this imposing residence stands in sheltered grounds on the outskirts of Huntly, commanding magnificent views of the countryside. Converted to an hotel in 1947, the present establishment is delightfully furnished throughout; décor, colour and modern facilities blending in perfect harmony. Central heating is installed throughout and one's ease may be taken in a spacious lounge or cosy cocktail bar. Food is excellent and varied and bedrooms attractively appointed. Salmon and trout fishing may be arranged and putting and croquet offer gentle diversion.

KILDRUMMY CASTLE HOTEL,
Kildrummy, By Alford,
Aberdeenshire   Tel: 033-65 288 (from Spring 1989: 09756-71288)*

Licensed; 16 bedrooms, all with private bathrooms; Historic interest; Children and dogs welcome; Car park; Alford 9 miles.

Set in the heart of Donside amidst cultivated gardens overlooking the ruins of the thirteenth century castle from which it takes its name, this warm and welcoming hotel is the ideal base from which to explore a countryside rich in history, natural beauty and sporting opportunity. There are over 70 castles in the region and approximately 30 golf courses within an hour's drive. Trout and salmon fishing is also available. This delightfully furnished hotel has elegant guest rooms all of which have a private bathroom, television, radio, telephone and several thoughtful extras. The restaurant has an excellent reputation for its fine food and service.

Please mention
Recommended COUNTRY HOTELS
when seeking refreshment or
accommodation at a Hotel
mentioned in these pages

Angus

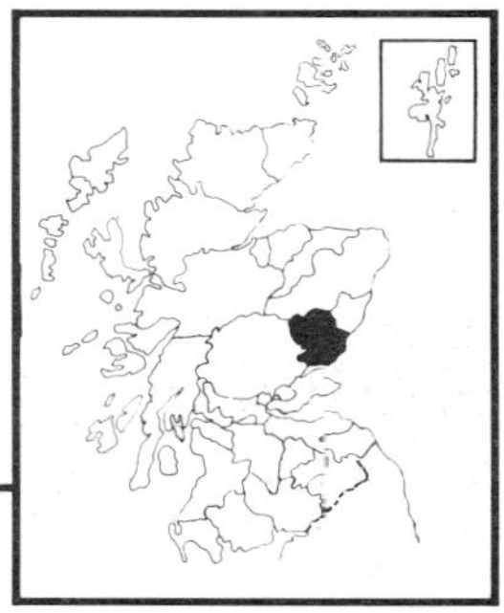

LETHAM GRANGE,
Colliston, By Arbroath,
Angus DD11 4RL

Tel: 024-189 373

Residential licence; 20 bedrooms, 17 with private bathrooms; Historic interest; Children welcome; Car park (50); London 494 miles, Perth 38, Dundee 20, Arbroath 4.

From Victorian mansion to luxury country hotel, Letham Grange has made a painless transition vastly assisted by imaginative refurbishing and its close associations with golf. Today, the lovely 300-acre wooded estate is the venue for all types of outdoor leisure activities including its own 18-hole championship standard golf course and a curling rink. The Sweep'n Swing bar lounge and restaurant overlooks the curling rink. With other golf courses at Rosemount, Carnoustie, St. Andrews and Gleneagles within easy reach, this superbly appointed hotel is ideal for active enthusiasts. Public and private rooms exude elegance and the cuisine is of high international standard.

PLEASE ENCLOSE A STAMPED
ADDRESSED ENVELOPE WHEN
WRITING TO ENQUIRE ABOUT
ACCOMMODATION FEATURED IN
THIS GUIDE

Argyll

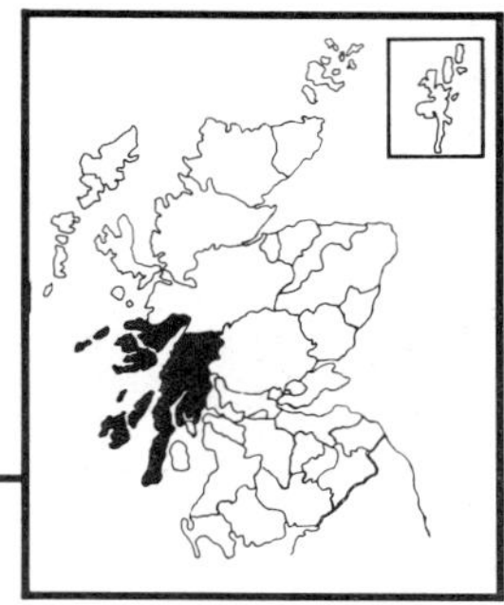

INVERCRERAN COUNTRY HOUSE HOTEL,
Glen Creran, Appin,
Argyll PA38 4BJ
Tel: 063-173 414/456

Residential licence; 7 bedrooms, all with private bathrooms; Car park; London 517 miles, Crianlarich 52, Fort William 25, Oban 18.

Situated in a most secluded part of the Highlands and built on a hillside overlooking Glen Creran with magnificent views making this the perfect location for guests seeking peace, relaxation, warmth and comfort. With luxurious facilities, Invercreran has an allure and tranquillity entirely in keeping with its setting. All bedrooms are well appointed, all with private facilities. Each room has a southern aspect with spectacular views. Our reception rooms and lounges are excellent; along with exquisite food and fine wines, the atmosphere and occasion are there to be enjoyed. This family run hotel endeavours to make your visit special and one to remember. *STB* 🌼 🌼 🌼 🌼 *Commended, Taste of Scotland recommended, Rosette awarded for cuisine.*

ISLE OF ERISKA HOTEL,
Ledaig, Connel,
Argyll PA37 15D
Tel: 0631-72 371*

Licensed; 16 bedrooms, all with private bathrooms; Historic interest; Children and dogs welcome; Car park; Oban 5 miles.

Romanticism and realism go hand in hand amidst the most grandiose scenery at this impressive and imposing castle-like hotel. Possessing all the attractions of remote seclusion, the hotel is set on a tiny island with a private vehicle bridge to the mainland. Here, in undisturbed serenity, one may be sure of delightfully furnished accommodation and traditional Scottish hospitality in the welcoming hands of Proprietors, Robin and Sheena Buchanan-Smith. The extensive attributes of the hotel are augmented by meticulous cuisine and cheery log fires. Children are welcome and for the active of all ages there are ponies, boats, all-weather courts and a croquet lawn.

TIRORAN HOUSE,
Isle of Mull,
Argyll

Tel: 068-15 232*

Restaurant and residential licence; 9 bedrooms, all with private bathrooms; Children over 10 years welcome; Car park.

Remote and romantic, this enchanting house is beautifully situated in twelve acres of lovely woodland gardens on the shores of tranquil Loch Scridain. This is truly the perfect retreat for lovers of peace, comfort and scenery of breathtaking splendour, to say nothing of a magnificent cuisine that will more than satisfy the most sharpened appetite. Dining by candlelight is a memorable experience. Five miles away is a National Trust property at Burgh where wild goats, golden eagles and other wildlife may be closely observed. There is golf at picturesque Tobermory and Craignure. Delightfully furnished, the little hotel has charming rooms and warmth provided by central heating and log fires.

ARDSHEAL HOUSE HOTEL,
Kentallen of Appin,
Argyll PA38 4BX

Tel: 063-174 227*

Restaurant and residential licence; 13 bedrooms, all with private bathrooms; Historic interest; Children and dogs welcome; Car park (16); Fort William 16 miles.

Approached down a mile-long drive that winds in and out of beautiful trees and meadows, Ardsheal tops a high peninsula that overlooks Loch Linnhe. This historic stone mansion, home of the Stewarts of Appin, is both imposing and gracious and the views all around are breathtaking. In keeping with its fame and antiquity (Ardsheal features in R.L. Stevenson's "Kidnapped") the house welcomes guests with traditional warmth. Excellent food is a major part of life here — the produce is local and the vegetables are home-grown. Fine wines, log fires and spacious, individually decorated rooms, each with a private bath, add to the comfort of guests. Sporting diversions include a tennis court and billiards room. Boating and riding are available locally.

KNIPOCH HOTEL,
By Oban,
Argyll

Tel: 085-26 251*

Licensed; 18 bedrooms, all with private bathrooms; Historic interest; Car park (40); Inveraray 48 miles.

For a memorable visit to the Western Highlands, this fine hotel is heartily recommended. Of some antiquity, being featured in historic records of the sixteenth century, this is the home of the Craig family who have modernised and extended the mainly Georgian building to offer amenities of considerable merit. The house has an imposing facade and is hard by the shores of Loch Feochan, some six miles south of Oban; a delectable situation, indeed. Beautifully furnished throughout, the hotel has well-appointed guest rooms, each with a private bathroom, heating, television, radio, telephone and magnificent views. Under the supervision of an expert chef, the food served is of high quality with Scottish specialities and seafood of prime interest.

KILCAMB LODGE HOTEL,
Strontian,
Argyll PH36 4HY
Tel: 0967 2257

Licensed; 9 bedrooms, all with private bathrooms; Historic interest; Children welcome; Car park; Inversanda 8 miles.

Wild and remote with beautiful beaches, the Ardnamurchan Peninsula is just the place to escape from the trammels of everyday life. Offering the very best of Highland hospitality, John and Suzanne Bradbury have transformed this attractive house into a first-class country hotel. Thirty acres of grounds surround this happy place which also has its own private beach on Loch Sunart. Central heating is installed throughout and public and private rooms are bright, cheerful and well equipped. Much attention is paid to the planning and presentation of the cuisine and the wine cellar complements the freshly-cooked food.

TAYCHREGGAN HOTEL,
Kilchrennan, By Taynuilt,
Argyll PA35 1HQ
Tel: 086-63 211*

Licensed; 16 bedrooms, 15 with private bathrooms; Historic interest; Children and dogs welcome; Car park; Crianlarich 29 miles, Oban 12.

Attractively arranged round a cobbled courtyard, Taychreggan can fairly claim to have one of the finest locations in Scotland. Set in 25 acres and facing southward over beautiful Loch Awe, the older part of the house was originally a drovers' inn and substantial additions have done nothing to mar its character. Good taste, simplicity and comfort is the theme of the interior. There are two sitting rooms overlooking the gardens and loch and a third public room for television and games. A pleasant bar opens on to a sunny, sheltered courtyard and regional and Continental dishes of high merit are served in the dining room. Boats may be hired from the hotel and riding, shooting and fishing may be organised nearby.

Other specialised

FHG PUBLICATIONS

* Recommended SHORT-BREAK HOLIDAYS IN BRITAIN   £2.95

* Recommended WAYSIDE INNS OF BRITAIN   £2.95

* PETS WELCOME!   £1.95

* BED AND BREAKFAST IN BRITAIN   £1.95

Published annually. Please add 30p postage (U.K. only) when ordering from the publishers:

FHG PUBLICATIONS LTD
Abbey Mill Business Centre, Seedhill,
Paisley, Renfrewshire PA1 1JN

Ayrshire

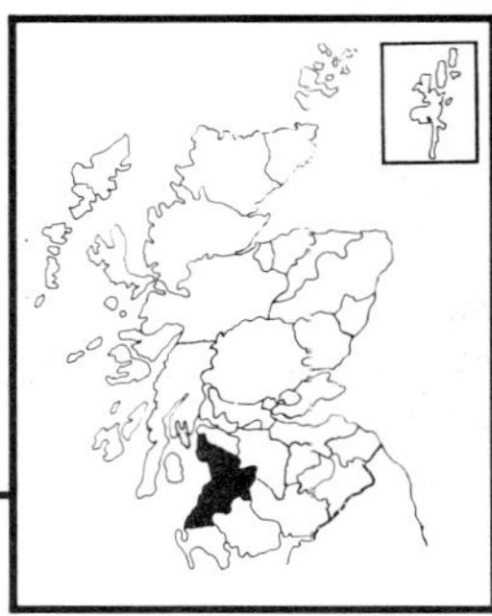

MANOR PARK HOTEL,
Skelmorlie,
Ayrshire PA17 5HE
Tel: 0475 520832*

Licensed; 23 bedrooms, all with private bathrooms or showers; Historic interest; Children welcome; Car park (150); Glasgow 31 miles, Paisley 25, Largs 3.

A beautiful country house in traditional Scottish baronial style, Manor Park is rich in historical associations, one of the most important being Winston Churchill and General Eisenhower planning the D-Day landings in the present Cowal Suite. Transformed into a hotel of impeccable style, it makes the most of its spacious rooms by well chosen furnishings and décor in keeping with its elegant past. Bedrooms are luxuriously furnished and include direct dial telephone and television, radio, alarm call, tea making facility and hair dryer, have private bathrooms and overlook the sea or the hotel's magnificent gardens of 15 acres. Here one may be certain of a really relaxing holiday with a willing staff on hand to serve one's every need. Good company may be found in the somewhat unusual cocktail bar and one may take one's ease in a spacious lounge and enjoy views which stretch across the Clyde estuary. With a fine reputation for its cuisine, the hotel has also become well known for its function facilities.

SUN COURT HOTEL,
Crosbie Road, Troon,
Ayrshire KA10 6HF
Tel: 0292 312727

Licensed; 20 bedrooms, all with private bathrooms; Historic interest; Children welcome; Car park (70); London 419 miles, Glasgow 32, Kilmarnock 10, Ayr 8.

That this fine, comfortable hotel is a mere chip shot away from a famous championship course and the fact that there are four other courses in Troon, speaks for itself, but the hotel provides opportunities for squash, tennis and, uniquely, real tennis as well. All the bedrooms have a private bathroom and overlook the Royal Troon golf course and the Firth of Clyde; all have colour television and teasmades. Four lounges epitomise quiet luxury and a bright and sizeable bar stocks a vast selection of whiskies and liqueurs. A prior visit here will heighten the enjoyment of the attractively presented à la carte and table d'hôte cuisine.

Berwickshire

CHIRNSIDE HALL COUNTRYHOUSE HOTEL,
Chirnside, Duns,
Berwickshire

Tel: 089-081 219

Restaurant licence; 15 bedrooms; Historic interest; Children and dogs welcome; Car park (30); Berwick-upon-Tweed 9 miles.

Chirnside Hall, a Victorian Mansion House set in 18 acres, offers something for everyone. Enjoy strolling through the gardens; putting, snooker and table tennis are some of our many facilities. Fishing, riding and golf nearby, with lovely beaches just a few miles away. In winter, relax by our open log fires. Chirnside Hall is a family run hotel providing morning coffee, high teas and evening meals. Open to non-residents, children welcome. Escape to the country . . . the Pine and Parker family welcome you to enchanted Chirnside Hall.

PURVES HALL HOTEL,
Greenlaw,
Berwickshire TD10 6UJ

Tel: 089-084 558

Licensed; 8 bedrooms, 2 with private bathrooms; Historic interest; Children and dogs welcome; Car park (30); Duns 7 miles.

A most attractive Edwardian country house, Purves Hall stands in 10 acres of woods, parkland and secluded gardens with magnificent views towards the Cheviot Hills. Warmly welcoming for guests of all ages, the hotel will appeal to family parties intent on touring the rewarding Border Country with its historic houses, softly rolling hills and quiet country roads. Public and private rooms are centrally heated and log fires add their cheer when the need arises. The hotel has limited but highly recommended accommodation, all guest rooms having en suite facilities, colour television, video and tea and coffee-makers. Personally prepared by Proprietors, Wing Commander and Mrs B.D. Everett and staff, excellent and varied meals are served in the Cheviot Restaurant. The hotel has an outdoor heated swimming pool, tennis court, riding stables, croquet and putting greens.

Dumfriesshire

MOFFAT HOUSE HOTEL,
Moffat,
Dumfriesshire DG10 9HL

Tel: 0683 20039*

Licensed; 16 bedrooms, all with private bathrooms; Historic interest; Children and dogs welcome; Car park; London 349 miles, Glasgow 54, Edinburgh 52, Carlisle 41.

This fine, Four Crown Commended country house hotel is set in two-and-a-half acres of gardens in the charming Dumfriesshire village of Moffat, just off the A74. An eighteenth century Adam mansion, it offers guests all the luxury and comforts which would originally have featured in a house of such distinction. All bedrooms are well equipped with colour TV, radio, direct dial telephone, central heating, and tea/coffee making tray. Light bar lunches and suppers are offered as well as an acclaimed à la carte dinner menu. Three day short breaks are available throughout the year, with prices from £85.50. The Reid family will be pleased to send their brochure.

RECOMMENDED SHORT-BREAK HOLIDAYS
IN BRITAIN

Introduced by John Carter, TV Holiday Expert and Journalist

Specifically designed to cater for the most rapidly growing sector of the holiday market in the UK. Illustrated details of hotels offering special 'Bargain Breaks' throughout the year.

Available from newsagents and bookshops or direct from the publishers:
£2.95 plus 30p postage.

FHG PUBLICATIONS LTD
Abbey Mill Business Centre, Seedhill,
Paisley, Renfrewshire PA1 1JN

Edinburgh & Lothians

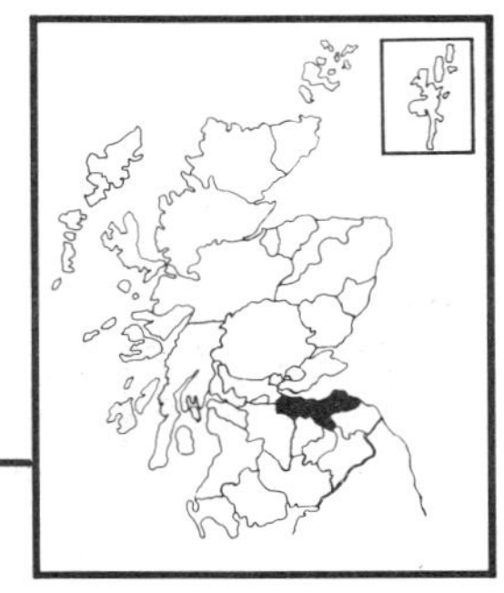

GREEN CRAIG HOUSE HOTEL,
Aberlady,
East Lothian EH32 0PY   Tel: 087-57 301

Licensed; 8 bedrooms, 5 with private bathrooms; Children welcome; Car park (25); North Berwick 6 miles.

On the shores of the Firth of Forth, Green Craig House commands sweeping views westward towards Edinburgh, only 20 minutes distant by road. Converted into a comfortable country hotel and restaurant as recently as 1982, this conveniently placed establishment in its 4 acres of secluded grounds, has already acquired a high reputation for its hospitality, cuisine and accommodation. Bedrooms, most with private bathrooms, overlook Gosford Bay with central heating, colour television and tea and coffee-making facilities and there are pleasing views of the gardens from the lounge where a log fire crackles in cool weather. Dining is a memorable experience, dishes being of French and Scottish origin with fresh local produce and home-made sweets.

DALHOUSIE CASTLE HOTEL,
Bonnyrigg, Edinburgh,
Mid Lothian EH19 3JB   Tel: 0875 20153

Licensed; 24 bedrooms, all with private bathrooms; Historic interest; Children welcome, dogs by arrangement; Car park; Dalkeith 2 miles.

During the 800 years of its history, Dalhousie Castle has been host to Edward I, Henry IV, Oliver Cromwell, Sir Walter Scott and Queen Victoria. Today, it is the family seat of the Ramsays of Dalhousie and has been lovingly converted into a luxurious hotel, whilst still retaining many of its finest features. Each of the splendid bedrooms has private bathroom, colour television, radio and telephone, and suites are also available. Public rooms are richly furnished in keeping with the period atmosphere and include a diningroom that must be unique, being converted from the ancient barrel-vaulted dungeons! The Castle is ideally located for touring the beautiful surrounding countryside, yet is only 20 minutes' drive from the centre of Edinburgh.

BORTHWICK CASTLE,
North Middleton, Gorebridge,
Midlothian EH23 4QY

Tel: 0875 20514

Restaurant licence; 10 bedrooms, all with private shower rooms; Historic interest; Children welcome; Car park; Edinburgh 15 miles, Dalkeith 4.

Once the refuge of the tragic Mary, Queen of Scots, this romantic and majestic castle with its fine baronial keep is one of the most historic buildings in Scotland and certainly one of the most interesting. Besieged by Oliver Cromwell's forces in the mid-seventeenth century, the Castle still bears the scars of cannon shot. These were turbulent times and legend has it that the early Borthwicks were not particularly well disposed towards their prisoners. A popular sport was to invite them to earn their liberty by jumping the 12-foot gap between the towers with hands tied behind their backs. Today, all is tranquil and guests may dine magnificently by candlelight in the beautiful Great Hall with its huge Gothic arch and minstrels' gallery and retire later to bedchambers furnished in period style but now blessed with en suite facilities. Moments of relaxation may be spent in the regal State Room with its arched windows, tapestries and small chapel. Other architectural features that will fascinate include the stone spiral staircases and the soaring twin towers that rise 110 feet from the dungeons to the battlements. The castle is surrounded by spacious grounds, ideal for a pre-dinner stroll. Riding, golf, shooting and excellent fishing may be arranged locally.

HOUSTOUN HOUSE,
Uphall,
West Lothian EH52 6JS

Tel: 0506 853831

Licensed; 30 bedrooms, all with private bathrooms; Historic interest; Children and dogs welcome; Car park (100); Edinburgh 13 miles.

With a gracious restaurant that provides some of the most interesting food in Scotland, this lovely, lofty, Lowland house offers a high standard of accommodation and food. Set in delightful grounds with an eighteen-hole golf course almost surrounding it, the house has a fascinating history yet today possesses all the comforts of the 20th century. Guest rooms are varied in their appeal, many of them having 18th-century panelling and several having four-poster beds. All the rooms have private bathrooms, central heating, telephone, radio and colour television. The Undercroft Bar is the setting for congenial drinking with a choice of malt whiskies from about 100 distilleries. A vast selection of wines from a fabulous cellar complements the fine cuisine in the three separate dining rooms. Uphall is a good centre for touring central Scotland as well as for seeing Edinburgh itself. *British Tourist Authority Commended Country Hotel, AA***, STB* 🌸 🌸 🌸 🌸.

> * The appearance of an asterisk after the telephone number indicates that the hotel in question is closed for a period during the winter months. Exact dates should be ascertained from the hotel itself.

Fife

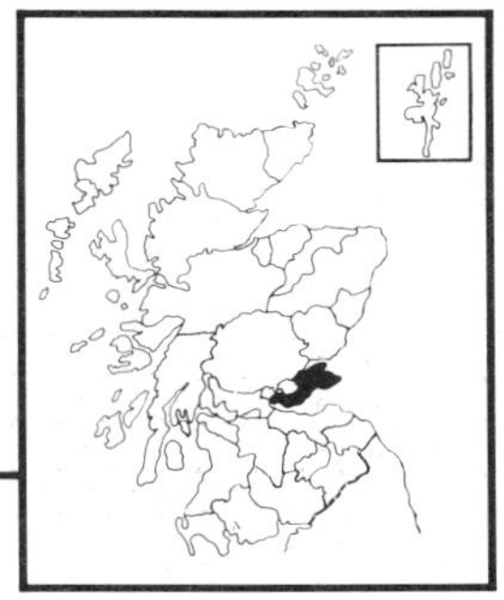

FERNIE CASTLE HOTEL,
Letham, Near Cupar,
Fife

Tel: 033-781 381*

Licensed; 16 bedrooms, all with private bathrooms; Historic interest; Children welcome; Car park (50); London 461 miles, Perth 19, Dundee 15, Cupar 5.

Well-known for the quality of its cuisine and wines, this is a small luxury hotel with a high standard of accommodation. It has an interesting history and it was first recorded in 1353 when it belonged as a castle to the Earl of Fife. The building still retains several architectural features worthy of inspection but the circular tower is a comparatively recent addition. All the rooms are magnificently appointed and the castle is centrally heated throughout. The diningroom with its gleaming silver, glass and candelabra, is a noble setting in which to enjoy the fine food. Good facilities exist nearby for golf and fishing. *AA***; STB* 🌷 🌷 🌷.

Inverness-shire

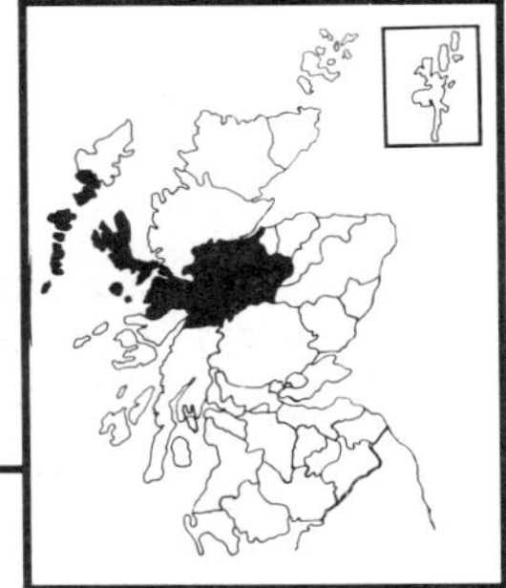

STAKIS FOUR SEASONS HOTEL,
Aviemore,
Inverness-shire PH22 1PF

Tel: 0479 810-681

Licensed; 90 bedrooms, all with private bathrooms; Dogs by arrangement; Car park (170); London 536 miles, Inverness 33, Grantown-on-Spey 15, Kingussie 12.

The proud boast of this hotel is that it is the finest in the lovely Spey Valley, and visitors will quickly realise its merit. Bedrooms are tastefully decorated and fitted to the highest of standards, distinctions which naturally extend to the public rooms. Guests may enjoy a relaxing drink in the elegant cocktail bar before dining in the opulence of the Four Seasons Restaurant. A quietly efficient staff is on hand as guests choose from menus offering the finest international cuisine and choice wine list. Regular dinner dances are held in the hotel, itself lying just minutes from the Aviemore Centre's year-round wealth of activity and entertainment.

ALLT-NAN-ROS HOTEL,
Onich, By Fort William,
Inverness-shire PH33 6RY

Tel: 085-53 210*

Licensed; 20 bedrooms, all with private facilities; Children and dogs welcome; Car park; Oban 39 miles, Fort William 10.

Named in Gaelic after the cascading stream that runs through the beautiful and colourful 4 acres of gardens, this fine hotel will hold special appeal for lovers of wild and romantic mountain and loch scenery. Situated on the A82 in the crofting village of Onich, Allt-nan-Ros is an imposing building of Victorian origin that has been modernised with skill and imagination. Guest rooms have magnificent views and are appointed with private bath and toilet facilities, radio, central heating, electric blankets and tea and coffee-makers. Under the attentive care of an expert chef, the cuisine is superbly prepared and presented from the full Scottish breakfast to dinner which features many imaginative specialities.

COZAC LODGE,
Glen Cannich, By Beauly,
Inverness-shire IV4 7LX

Tel: 045-65 263*

Restaurant and residential licence; 7 bedrooms, all with private bathrooms; Historic interest; Car park (12); Inverness 13 miles.

Warm and friendly and of great character, this one-time shooting lodge lies in the heart of the Highlands in Glen Cannich, famous for its red deer and other interesting wildlife. The situation is both tranquil and spectacular and the views across Loch Sealbanach to the Affric Mountains are breathtaking. A country home in the truest sense, the hotel has comfortable lounges and luxuriously-appointed guest rooms, each with its own bath or shower, WC and colour television. The tangy Highland air promotes hearty appetites which are well satisfied by the first-class and interesting cuisine, much use being made of fresh local produce in company with carefully selected wines.

CULLODEN HOUSE HOTEL,
Inverness,
Inverness-shire IV1 2NZ

Tel: 0463 790461 Telex: 75402

Fax: 0463 792181

Licensed; 20 bedrooms, all with private bathrooms; Historic interest; Children and dogs welcome; Car park (50); Nairn 16 miles, Dingwall 14.

Starting life as a Jacobean castle, this handsome mansion has a tradition of lavish hospitality that spans hundreds of years. Among its famous visitors was Bonnie Prince Charlie who fought his last battle by the park walls. Beautifully decorated public and private rooms make the most of their historically interesting features but contemporary amenities have been skilfully introduced to delight present-day guests. Furnishings represent the ultimate in comfort with the opulence of the ages softened by warm and cleverly-planned colour schemes. Each bedroom has a private bath and shower, television and direct-dial telephone; four-poster rooms are available and one with a jacuzzi. Excellent meals, specialising in game, salmon and country house fare, are served in a charming Adam dining room and backed by efficient and unobtrusive service. Nestling amidst the elegant lawns, stately oak and beech trees of the 40 acres of grounds, the habitat of deer and wild-fowl, this enlightened hotel is just five miles from Inverness Airport and is a peerless touring centre for the Highlands. The hotel has its own helipad and generous parking and leisure facilities include a hard tennis court, full-size snooker table, sauna and solarium, whilst opportunities exist nearby for golf, fishing, sailing and shooting.

THE LODGE ON THE LOCH,
Creag Dhu, Onich, By Fort William,
Inverness-shire PH33 6RY

Tel: 085-53 237/238
Telex: 94013696; Fax: 08552 629

*Licensed; 20 bedrooms, 17 with private bathrooms; Children and dogs welcome; Car park (25);
Edinburgh 120 miles, Glasgow 93, Oban (ferry) 39, Fort William 10, Ballachulish 3.*

The Lodge On The Loch enjoys one of the most romantic and spectacular lochside settings, in a land famed for its splendid scenery. Visitors to this lovely spot will enjoy a really warm Highland welcome, where old world standards of hospitality unite with modern comforts to ensure a restful, peaceful stay. All bedrooms are individually designed and furnished and feature fine woven fabrics from the Islands. The public rooms are cheered by log fires and the hotel is justly proud of its fine Highland cuisine with local seafood, salmon, trout, and venison; or you may prefer to try the wholefood vegetarian menu and irresistible home baking. *Recommended by leading food and accommodation guides; STB* ❀ ❀ ❀ ❀ *Commended.*

Isle of Skye

KINLOCH LODGE,
Sleat,
Isle of Skye IV43 8QY

Tel: 047-13 214/333*

*Restaurant and residential licence; 10 bedrooms, all with private bathrooms; Historic interest;
Children over 8 years welcome; Car park (20).*

Home of Lord and Lady MacDonald, this elegant stone building was erected in 1680 and was, at one time, a shooting lodge. Now fulfilling its role as a first-class country retreat of distinction, Kinloch Lodge is delightfully remote and the ideal place in which to relax and enjoy dramatic scenery, excellent food and service and, above all, utter tranquillity. Fringed by the sea on two sides, this is a friendly place with open fires, individually decorated guest rooms, plenty of quiet diversions and panoramic views. The cuisine, in the expert hands of Lady MacDonald, is of the highest order with the accent on non-additive food. Everything is home-made from the breakfast scones to the delicious after-dinner fudge.

Kirkcudbright

BALCARY BAY HOTEL,
Auchencairn, Near Castle Douglas,
Kirkcudbrightshire DG7 1QZ

Tel: 055-664 217*

Licensed; 14 bedrooms, 12 with private bathrooms; Historic interest; Children and dogs welcome; Car park (50); Edinburgh 94 miles, New Galloway 22, Dumfries 21, Gatehouse-of-Fleet 19.

Whether it be relaxing on the cocktail bar patio overlooking the bay, imbibing in the Cave Bar created from the house's cellars or reclining on a four-poster bed, visitors will reflect that their choice of the Balcary Bay Hotel was a wise one. The personal supervision of Resident Owners Ron and Joan Lamb and their son Graeme ensures that efficiency is matched by friendliness and that a family atmosphere prevails. Imaginative cuisine based on local delicacies. Sporting opportunities abound in the area, while the hotel's billiard room provides an alternative to outdoor pursuits. *AA***, RAC***, STB* 🌼🌼🌼🌼 *Commended.*

CULGRUFF HOUSE HOTEL,
Crossmichael, Castle Douglas,
Kirkcudbrightshire DG7 3BB

Tel: 055-667 230*

Licensed; 17 bedrooms, 4 with private bathrooms; Children and dogs welcome; Car park; Dumfries 18 miles, Kirkcudbright 10.

Former home of the Duchess of Grafton, this imposing baronial mansion stands above the village of Crossmichael with lovely views extending across the Ken Valley. With many fascinating architectural features, including the panelled hallway, high-vaulted lounge and the fine figured ceiling in the conservatory lounge, the house is an excellent touring holiday base for Galloway, Burns Country and the Borders. Comfortably appointed throughout, Culgruff stands in attractive grounds of 35 acres and for the active sportsman there are facilities for tennis, riding, golf and bird watching within easy reach as well as boating and watersports on the loch or sea.

NOTE

All the information in this book is given in good faith in the belief that it is correct. However, the publishers cannot guarantee the facts given in these pages, neither are they responsible for changes in policy, ownership or terms that may take place after the date of going to press. Readers should always satisfy themselves that the facilities they require are available and that the terms, if quoted, still apply.

CLONYARD HOUSE HOTEL,
Colvend, Dalbeattie,
Kirkcudbrightshire DG5 4QW

Tel: 055-663 372

Licensed; 10 bedrooms, 7 with private bathrooms; Children and dogs welcome; Car park (40); Dumfries 13 miles.

Embowered by trees that are a feature of the 7 acres of grounds, this fine, upstanding house will appeal to family parties. Here, children may play in safety whilst parents consider the possibilities of excellent salmon and trout fishing and golf on any of four nearby courses. Other amenities to attract include a convivial cocktail bar, wholesome cuisine and delightfully furnished accommodation with a baby-listening service. Bedrooms have colour television, radio, direct-dial telephone and tea and coffee making facilities and many of them have bathroom en suite with several situated on the ground floor. Recommended for a rewarding country-by-sea holiday, Clonyard House is quietly placed on the Solway Coast between Rockcliffe and Kippford.

Nairnshire

NEWTON HOTEL,
Nairn,
Nairnshire IV12 4RX

Tel: 0667 53144

Licensed; 44 bedrooms, all with private bathrooms; Historic interest; Children and dogs welcome; Car park; Inverness 16 miles.

An excellent centre for touring Royal Deeside, Loch Ness and the Highlands, this delightful and impressive hotel is of special appeal to sports enthusiasts for a championship golf course is only a few hundred yards away and stalking, fishing, squash and other activities may be arranged locally. An imposing combination of Georgian and Scottish baronial styles, this fine establishment has 27 acres of secluded grounds which incorporate a tennis court and 9-hole putting green and there are magnificent views over the Moray Firth. Approaching the hotel via a tree-lined drive from the Inverness-Aberdeen road, guests will immediately appreciate the elegance of period furniture and subtle decor which recalls the opulence of Victorian days.

Peeblesshire

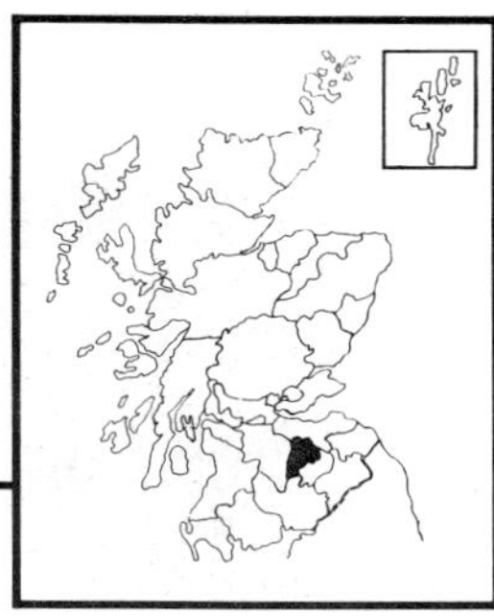

VENLAW CASTLE HOTEL,
Peebles,
Peebles-shire EH45 8QG

Tel: 0721 20384*

Licensed; 12 bedrooms, 9 with private bathrooms; Historic interest; Children and dogs welcome; Car park (20); Galashiels 19 miles.

Impressive yet warmly welcoming, this building, with its towers and gables, is a fine example of architecture in the Scottish baronial style. Dating from 1782 and now a splendid country retreat serving tourists to the Lowlands and Border Country, Venlaw stands in 6 acres of tranquil, wooded grounds and within, is full of character with spacious and elegant rooms now blessed with attractive contemporary comforts. Bedrooms are delightfully appointed, several being available with bathrooms en suite. Backed by attentive service, the cuisine features fresh local produce and the library cocktail bar, with its open fire, is a convivial meeting place.

Please mention
Recommended COUNTRY HOTELS
when seeking refreshment or
accommodation at a Hotel
mentioned in these pages

TWEED VALLEY HOTEL AND RESTAURANT,
Walkerburn, Near Peebles,
Peeblesshire EH43 6AA

Tel: 089-687 636

Licensed; 16 bedrooms, all with private bathrooms; Historic interest; Children and dogs welcome; Car park (35); Innerleithen 2 miles.

As a centre for touring the beautiful Border Country, this privately-owned Edwardian country house hotel and restaurant on the River Tweed is a natural choice. Quiet, friendly and superbly appointed, the hotel has a noteworthy reputation for good food and is a member of the Taste of Scotland scheme, for traditional Scottish food with salmon, trout, venison and other game dishes available in season as well as 'sizzle grill' bar lunches. Log fires augment the central heating in providing the warmest of welcomes. There is a sauna and mini-gym and rooms all have private bath or shower, toilet, colour television, hairdryer and direct-dial telephone. Many sporting activities are organised by the hotel, including golf, fishing, riding, walking, bird watching, shooting and stalking. There are tartan, wool and cashmere shopping discounts for guests. *STB* 🌺 🌺 🌺 🌺 *Commended. AA Hospitality Service Award. RAC***.*

FOR THE MUTUAL GUIDANCE
OF GUEST AND HOST

Every year literally thousands of holidays, short-breaks and overnight stops are arranged through our guides, the vast majority without any problems at all. In a handful of cases, however, difficulties do arise about bookings, which often could have been prevented from the outset.

It is important to remember that when accommodation has been booked, both parties — guests and hosts — have entered into a form of contract. We hope that the following points will provide helpful guidance.

GUESTS: When enquiring about accommodation, be as precise as possible. Give exact dates, numbers in your party and the ages of any children. State the number and type of rooms wanted and also what catering you require — bed and breakfast, full board, etc. Make sure that the position about evening meals is clear — and about pets, reductions for children or any other special points.

Read our reviews carefully to ensure that the proprietors you are going to contact can supply what you want. Ask for a letter confirming all arrangements, if possible.

If you have to cancel, do so as soon as possible. Proprietors do have the right to retain deposits and under certain circumstances to charge for cancelled holidays if adequate notice is not given and they cannot re-let the accommodation.

HOSTS: Give details about your facilities and about any special conditions. Explain your deposit system clearly and arrangements for cancellations, charges, etc, and whether or not your terms include VAT.

If for any reason you are unable to fulfil an agreed booking without adequate notice, you may be under an obligation to arrange alternative suitable accommodation or to make some form of compensation.

While every effort is made to ensure accuracy, we regret that FHG Publications cannot accept responsibility for errors, omissions or misrepresentation in our entries or any consequences thereof. Prices in particular should be checked because we go to press early. We will follow up complaints but cannot act as arbiters or agents for either party.

Perthshire

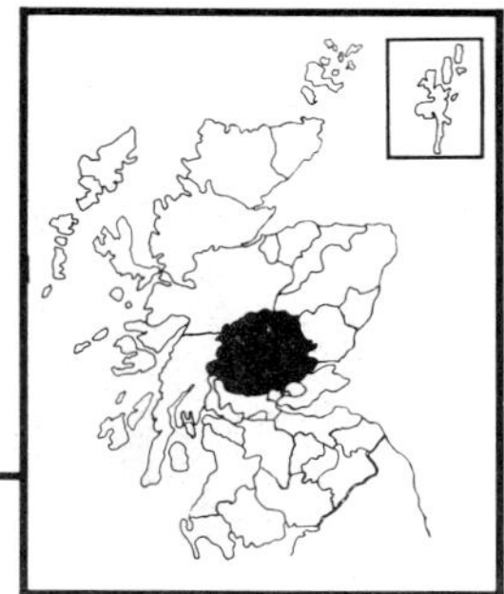

ALTAMOUNT HOUSE HOTEL,
Coupar Angus Road, Blairgowrie,
Perthshire PH10 6JN

Tel: 0250 3512*

Licensed; 7 bedrooms, all with private facilities; Historic interest; Car park (40); Perth 16 miles.

Charmingly refurbished and opened as an hotel in 1980, Altamount is a splendid Georgian country house that has already achieved a fine reputation for its furnishings, comfort and appetising Scottish cuisine under the enthusiastic supervision of Proprietors Ritchie and Sue Russell. Set in 6 acres of woodland and gardens in one of Scotland's favourite tourist centres, the house has a warm and welcoming atmosphere conjured up by original Adam fireplaces and corniced ceilings to which wood panelling, elegant furniture and subdued lighting have been introduced to maximum effect. The cuisine is cause for celebration, imaginative and beautifully-prepared dishes being presented to the accompaniment of silver cutlery and crystal glassware. Morning coffee is served before a log fire in the lounge; afternoon teas are also available and the traditional Sunday lunch is a popular occasion. The lounge bar proves to be a convivial meeting place and an attractive room is set aside for small private functions. After the activities of the day, sweet and satisfying repose is assured in guest rooms with private facilities, colour television, electric blankets and other thoughtful extras. Full central heating is installed. There are several well-known golf courses in the area and the River Tay offers excellent salmon and trout fishing.

Available from most bookshops, the 1989 edition of THE GOLF GUIDE covers details of every UK golf course – well over 2000 entries – for holiday or business golf. Hundreds of hotel entries offer convenient accommodation, accompanying details of the courses – the 'pro', par score, length etc.

Sandy Lyle features on the front cover with golfing editorial from the Professional Golfers Association who also endorse the guide.

£4.95 from bookshops or £5.50 including postage from FHG Publications, Abbey Mill Business Centre, Paisley PA1 1JN.

ROMAN CAMP HOTEL,
Callander,
Perthshire FK17 8BG

Tel: 0877 30003*

Licensed; 14 bedrooms, all with private bathrooms or shower rooms; Historic interest; Well-behaved children and dogs welcome; Car park; Glasgow 35 miles, Stirling 14.

Sharply reminiscent of a miniature chateau, this splendid country house dates back to 1625 and today exudes a warm and friendly atmosphere due, in no small part, to its courteous and efficient staff. Apart from its ruggedly idyllic setting, the hotel is widely acclaimed for the high standard of its food which is prepared under the direct supervision of the Chef-Proprietor, Sami Denzler, and complemented by a superb range of wines selected by Pat Denzler. Tastefully furnished guest rooms all have private bath/shower, colour television, radio, direct-dial telephone, hair-dryer and tea and coffee-making facilities. Fishing on the River Teith, which runs through the hotel grounds, is free to residents and Callander Golf Course is only half-a-mile away.

STAKIS DUNBLANE HYDRO,
Dunblane,
Perthshire FK15 0HG

Tel: 0786 822551

Licensed; 224 bedrooms, all with private bathrooms; Children welcome, dogs by arrangement; Car park (350); London 425 miles, Glasgow 32, Perth 28, Stirling 6.

The splendid Victorian façade of this magnificently set hotel is just a foretaste of the luxury to follow. Each bedroom – including three suites – has private facilities, TV, radio, telephone, and tea/coffee making facilities, with extras like trouser press, hairdryer, morning paper, fresh fruit, and shortbread. The Balmoral Restaurant maintains the highest standards of cuisine, with traditional Taste of Scotland dishes a feature. Dances, ceilidhs, and evening entertainment is always available. The hotel's leisure club has an indoor pool, sauna, solarium and gym, while outdoor facilities aplenty are available, including putting, all-weather tennis courts, and a jogging trail. Riding, shooting, fishing, and golf may also be arranged nearby.

CROMLIX HOUSE,
Kinbuck, Dunblane,
Perthshire FK15 9JT

Tel: 0786 822125*

Restaurant and residential licence; 14 bedrooms, all with private bathrooms; Historic interest; Children and dogs welcome; Car park (150); Stirling 6 miles.

As imposing inside as it is from external appearance, the late-Victorian Cromlix House revels in its furnishings with fine prints and paintings, porcelain, silver and glassware acquired over centuries. Set in 5000 acres rich in wildlife in the heart of Perthshire, the house has been much changed since its early years without affecting its aura of warmth and style. Now with central heating boosted by open fires, the hotel epitomises real Scottish hospitality with luxury suites and bedrooms all having private bathrooms.

STAKIS DUNKELD HOUSE HOTEL,
Dunkeld,
Perthshire PH8 0HX

Tel: 035-02 771

Licensed; 101 bedrooms, all with private bathrooms; Historical interest; Dogs by arrangement; Car park (40); London 463 miles, Perth 15, Pitlochry 13.

When the seventh Duke of Atholl decided to build a home for his Duchess, he chose the most spectacular setting he could find and constructed the magnificent building that is now Dunkeld House Hotel. Surrounding the house are over 100 acres of shrubs, flowers, rhododendrons, huge trees and splendid walks as well as a private two-mile stretch of the River Tay, famed for salmon fishing. Accommodation and cuisine are of the high standard that one would expect at a top-class country hotel and service is exemplary. Ideal for leisure and sporting activities. The hotel is an excellent base for those wishing to explore this beautiful and interesting 'Macbeth' area of Scotland.

LOCHEARNHEAD HOTEL,
Lochearnhead,
Perthshire

Tel: 05673 229*

Licensed; 12 bedrooms, some with private bathrooms; Children and dogs welcome; Car park; Edinburgh 65 miles, Glasgow 50, Aberfeldy 30, Crieff 19.

On the edge of Loch Earn with spectacular views over hills and glens, the hotel is admirably situated for a touring holiday and has all manner of watersports within a stone's throw. The menu is good and varied, and guests may sample both traditional fare and Cordon Bleu dishes in the elegant, candlelit diningroom. Children are warmly welcomed, and a special menu is available for them. The hotel is centrally heated and decor and furnishings throughout reflect the good taste of proprietor Angus Cameron. On chilly evenings a crackling log fire burns brightly in the lounge, and the pleasant Bistro Bar is another popular gathering place. Also luxury self-catering accommodation available.

MANSEWOOD COUNTRY HOUSE,
Lochearnhead,
Perthshire FK19 8NS

Tel: 05673 213

Residential licence; 7 bedrooms, 4 with private bathrooms; Historic interest; Children welcome; Car park (10); Perth 37 miles, Stirling 30.

Mansewood Country House is a seven bedroomed hotel set in the heart of some of the most beautiful touring country in Scotland. It is approximately 200 years old and was once, as the names implies, the manse for the church opposite. The emphasis here is on informality, and all guests are assured of a warm and friendly welcome. This atmosphere is enhanced by the comfort of the surroundings: the diningroom has an open log fire, and the lounge a wood burning stove, while the small sun lounge leads to a friendly bar for guests' before and after dinner drinks. Bedrooms are cosy and welcoming and all have double glazing, central heating and electric blankets. Food, too, is of a high quality. An excellent touring base, Mansewood is also within easy reach of several golf courses where visitors are welcome, being just outside the village of Lochearnhead, surrounded by trees and hills, yet within easy walking distance of the busy watersports area of Loch Earn. Short breaks available. Your hosts: Sue and Jeff Jeffery. *AA*; FHG Award winner 1986; Les Routiers.*

KINGS OF KINLOCH HOTEL,
Meigle,
Perthshire PH12 8QX

Tel: 082-84 273

Licensed; 8 bedrooms, 2 with private bathrooms; Historic interest; Children and dogs welcome; Car park (70); Dundee 13 miles.

All elegance and style, this late 18th century house is perfectly placed for those with sporting facilities and Scotland's history in mind. There are several good golf courses nearby and the shooting for grouse, pheasant and deer is excellent as is the fishing for salmon and trout. Set in attractive grounds of 15 acres, the hotel is also conveniently near Glamis Castle, Scone Palace and other places associated with Caledonia's heritage. Enjoying splendid views, the bedrooms are, in the main, spacious as well as being tastefully and efficiently appointed. With the accent on comfort, cleanliness and good service, the hotel has a growing reputation for its cuisine and fine wines.

PINE TREES HOTEL,
Strathview Terrace, Pitlochry,
Perthshire PH16 5QR

Tel: 0796 2121*

Licensed; 20 bedrooms; 19 with private bathrooms; Children welcome; Car park (40); Perth 27 miles.

Centrally placed for a comprehensive Scottish touring holiday, Pitlochry has countless attractions of its own, not least this comfortably-furnished hotel. Mr. and Mrs. J.T. MacLellan and their family extend a warm welcome to guests who will find the standards of accommodation, cuisine and service well beyond expectations. A peaceful atmosphere pervades this lovely hotel and the bedrooms all have private bathroom or shower, colour television and tea and coffee-making facilities, whilst the restful public rooms are decorated with an eye to harmonious colour schemes. In an area of breathtaking scenic beauty, the hotel has a putting green and the Pitlochry Golf Course is nearby. Fishing and shooting may be arranged by prior booking.

THE MURRAYSHALL COUNTRY HOUSE HOTEL,
Scone, Perth,
Perthshire

Tel: 0738 51171 Fax: 0738 52595

Licensed; 19 bedrooms, 16 with private bathrooms; Children and dogs welcome; Car park (100); Perth 2 miles.

The Murrayshall is a friendly country house-style hotel set in beautiful surroundings in the heart of Scotland. The hotel's 19 bedrooms are well equipped. An award winning chef creates dishes of a Scottish flavour with just a hint of modern French cuisine, which is served in the Old Masters' Restaurant, where a pianist/harpist plays most evenings. The hotel is the venue for several leisure activities with its own 18 hole, par 73 golf course, tennis courts, bowling and croquet available. Fishing and shooting by arrangement nearby. The historic Scone Palace lies nearby, as does a whisky distillery and Caithness Glass.

BALCRAIG HOUSE HOTEL,
By Scone, Perth,
Perthshire PH2 7PG

Tel: 0738 51123

Licensed; 10 bedrooms, all with private bathrooms; Historic interest; Children and dogs welcome; Car park (30); Forfar 28 miles, Perth 2.

With views across the countryside to the fine city of Perth, Balcraig House stands at the foot of the Sidlaw Hills, convenient for touring and with many sporting opportunities close at hand. The hotel has extensive gardens and guests may play tennis on the all-weather court, croquet on the lawns or go pony trekking through the surrounding woodlands. There are several championship golf courses nearby and fishing, stalking and shooting may also be arranged. Victorian in origin, the hotel is delightfully appointed in an amalgam of old and new. Bedrooms have en suite bathrooms, colour television, radio, trouser press, hairdryer, direct-dial telephone and numerous subtle extras, not least the exquisite hand-painted wall murals. Crystal chandeliers, log fires, fine pictures and antiques promote a feeling of well-being, a mood completed by excellent, well-presented cuisine and service. Meals are served in a Victorian-style conservatory diningroom overlooking the gardens. Very good facilities for private functions and business meetings which can be arranged under the personal supervision of the proprietors.

Renfrewshire

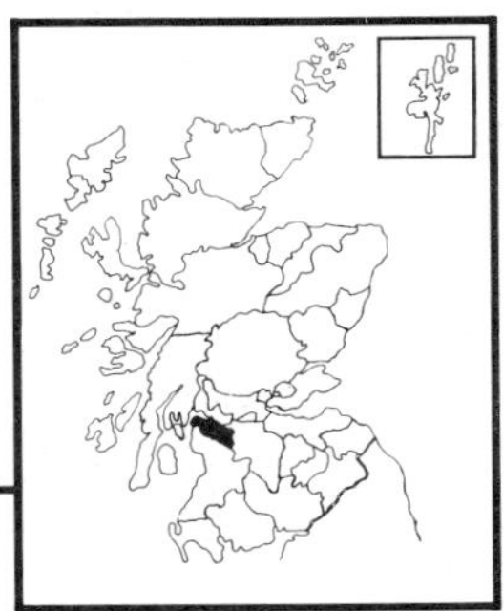

STAKIS GANTOCK HOTEL,
Cloch Road, Gourock,
Renfrewshire PA15 1AR

Tel: 0475 34671

Licensed; 101 bedrooms, all with private bathrooms; Children welcome, dogs by arrangement; Car park (220); London 432 miles, Glasgow 27, Largs 15, Greenock 4.

Set against a woodland backdrop and commanding magnificent views across the Firth of Clyde to the Argyll hills beyond, this is a superb base for touring Burns Country and the West Coast. Accommodation is of the highest standard, with many thoughtful extras provided. A choice of bars – including the friendly Gallery Bar with its fine views – allows guests to enjoy a drink before dining in Chandlers Restaurant, with menus to whet the appetite and a view to capture the imagination. The hotel's Leisure Club offers superb facilities, including pool and whirlpool, fitness equipment, sunbed, sauna, and two all weather tennis courts.

Ross-shire

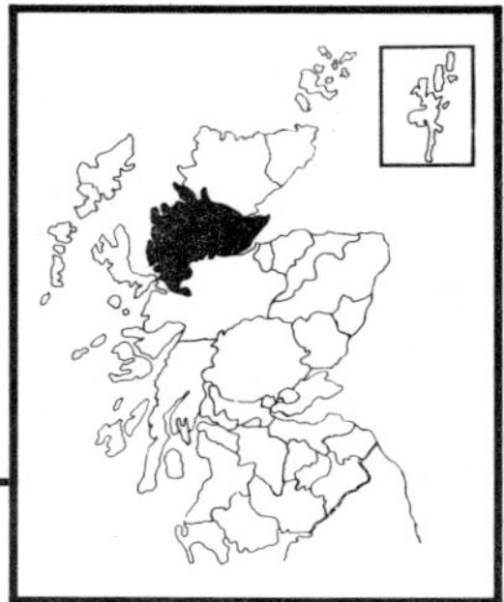

LEDGOWAN LODGE HOTEL,
Achnasheen, Wester Ross,
Ross-shire IV22 2EJ   Tel: 044-588 252*

Licensed; 15 bedrooms, all with private bathrooms; Children welcome; Car park; Inverness 42 miles, Dingwall 30.

The wholesome comforts offered by this charming and warmly welcoming hotel go hand in hand with its convenience as a touring base from which to discover the scenic grandeur of North Scotland. To the east of this former shooting lodge is Loch Ness and Glen Affric and to the west is the road to Skye, lovely Loch Maree and the sub-tropical gardens at Inverewe. All around is magnificent mountain scenery and the Ben Eighe Nature Reserve is only ten miles away. The hotel is beautifully appointed and is noted for its excellent catering and service. Children are welcome and a special restaurant menu is available to them.

TIR-ALUINN HOTEL,
Leckmelm, Loch Broom, Ullapool
Ross-shire IV23 2RJ   Tel: 0854 2074*

Hotel licence; 16 bedrooms, 3 with private bathrooms; Children and dogs welcome; Car park (30); Dingwall 42 miles, Ullapool 4.

On a small and remote promontory overlooking Loch Broom, the homely Tir-Aluinn Hotel is a quiet holiday venue in 20 acres of gardens, surrounded by Highland scenery at its grandest. The hotel has its own jetty and there are facilities for swimming, boating and fishing, whilst climbing, pony trekking and motor trips are also catered for. With lovely views, guest rooms are comfortably furnished with private bathrooms available and terms for accommodation and food are most reasonable. Dinner presents a choice of three main dishes regularly featuring home-cooked beef, venison, lamb, pork and fresh salmon.

---

* The appearance of an asterisk after the telephone number indicates that the hotel in question is closed for a period during the winter months. Exact dates should be ascertained from the hotel itself.

Roxburghshire

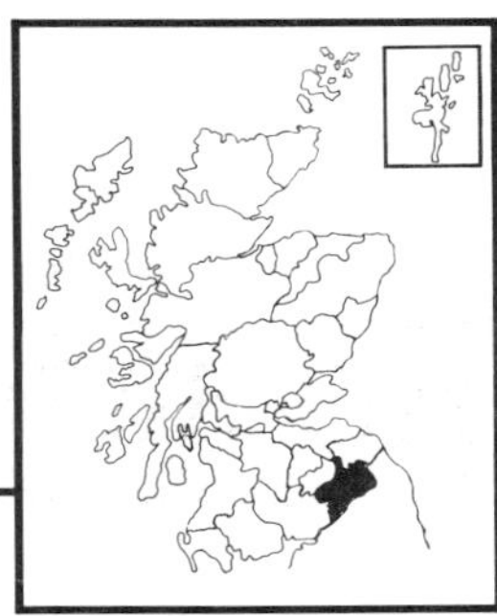

GLENFRIARS HOTEL,
The Friars, Jedburgh,
Roxburghshire TD8 6BN

Tel: 0835 62000

Restaurant and residential licence; 6 bedrooms, all with private bathrooms; Historic interest; Children and dogs welcome; Car park (8); Edinburgh 48 miles, Kelso 11.

As a recommended centre for touring the romantic Border Country, this recently-opened hotel overlooks the pleasant town of Jedburgh and offers a high degree of modern comfort with excellent Scottish cuisine giving further cause for consideration. Special diets are catered for and there is a good selection of wines and malt whiskies. The atmosphere is warm and friendly and guest rooms have splendid facilities, each appointed with a private bathroom, television, electric blanket and tea and coffee-maker. Activities to enjoy in the soft-rolling countryside include walking, fishing for salmon and trout, golf and pony trekking and there are countless historic buildings in the vicinity.

RECOMMENDED SHORT-BREAK HOLIDAYS
IN BRITAIN

Introduced by John Carter, TV Holiday Expert and Journalist

Specifically designed to cater for the most rapidly growing sector of the holiday market in the UK. Illustrated details of hotels offering special 'Bargain Breaks' throughout the year.

Available from newsagents and bookshops or direct from the publishers: £2.95 plus 30p postage.

FHG PUBLICATIONS LTD
Abbey Mill Business Centre, Seedhill,
Paisley, Renfrewshire PA1 1JN

Selkirkshire

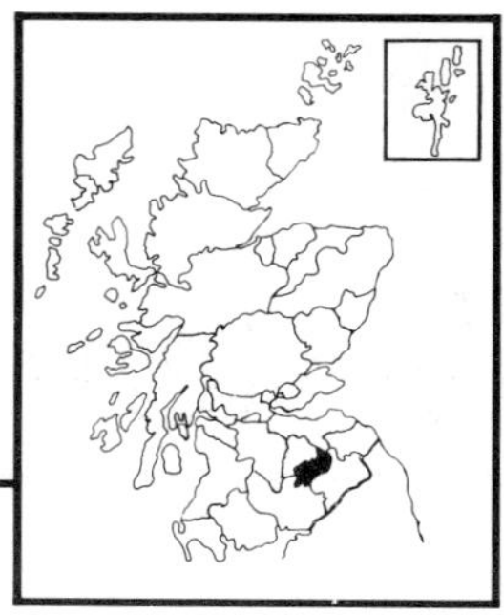

WOODBURN HOUSE HOTEL,
Selkirk,
Selkirkshire TD7 1AL

Tel: 0750 20816

Licensed; 10 bedrooms, 7 with private bathrooms; Historic interest; Children and dogs welcome; Car park (45); London 364 miles, Edinburgh 40, Galashiels 6.

Specialising in traditional home cooking and with guest rooms representing the ultimate in comfort, this attractive Victorian mansion is a fine holiday base for exploring the Scottish Borders. Located at the junction of the Ettrick, Yarrow and Tweed Valleys and in four acres of garden, the hotel is within easy reach of many places of natural beauty and historic interest. For the active sportsman, private salmon and trout fishing may be enjoyed as well as deer stalking, shooting, golf and horse riding. Stabling is available in the grounds for guests wishing to bring their own horses. Warm and welcoming, the hotel is a tranquil place in which to relax with a convivial bar for guests' enjoyment.

PLEASE ENCLOSE A STAMPED
ADDRESSED ENVELOPE WHEN
WRITING TO ENQUIRE ABOUT
ACCOMMODATION FEATURED IN
THIS GUIDE

Western Isles

SCARISTA HOUSE,
Isle of Harris,
Outer Hebrides

Tel: 085-985 238*

Residential licence; 7 bedrooms, all with private bathrooms; Historic interest; Children over 8 and dogs welcome; Car park (10); Stornoway 37 miles.

Really away from it all amidst the maritime scenery of the Western Isles, this charming Georgian house was once the principal Church of Scotland manse for Harris. Facing the Atlantic and overlooking an expanse of beach, the little hotel offers many comforts for the holidaymaker seeking complete change. Peat fires in the sitting room augment the central heating and there is a sunny drawing room and well-stocked library with no television or radio. Bedrooms are attractively furnished with bathrooms en suite. An important feature is the cuisine with seafood and local produce figuring prominently. Meals are beautifully presented and served in a charming candlelit dining room with fine wines and spirits in support.

NOTE

All the information in this book is given in good faith in the belief that it is correct. However, the publishers cannot guarantee the facts given in these pages, neither are they responsible for changes in policy, ownership or terms that may take place after the date of going to press. Readers should always satisfy themselves that the facilities they require are available and that the terms, if quoted, still apply.

Wigtownshire

HILL OF BURNS,
Hill Street, Creetown,
Wigtownshire DG8 7HF

Tel: 067-182 487*

Licensed; 8 bedrooms, 6 with private bathrooms; Historic interest; Children welcome; Car park (10); London 387 miles, Glasgow 93, Carlisle 80, Newton Stewart 7.

Hill of Burns is an eighteenth century country house hotel set in eight acres of lovely woodland and gardens, overlooking the Cree Estuary and Wigtown Bay. It is ideally situated to allow guests to take advantage of the splendid opportunities for sport nearby, with good fishing and golf easily available. Walking, pony trekking and bird watching are also available nearby. The hotel provides a restful haven to which to return at the end of the day, with 8 individually decorated and comfortable bedrooms, and a relaxing diningroom offering the best of fresh local produce and fine wines. Creetown itself is famed for local crafts, while the archaeological dig at Whithorn is only 30 minutes away. *STB* 👑 👑.

Please mention
Recommended COUNTRY HOTELS
when seeking refreshment or
accommodation at a Hotel
mentioned in these pages

MAP SECTION

The following seven pages of maps indicate the main cities, towns and holiday centres of Britain. Space obviously does not permit every location featured in this book to be included but the approximate position may be ascertained by using the distance indications quoted and the scale bars on the maps.

Map 1

A B C D E F
1 2 3 4
Stafford
Shrewsbury
Wellington
Wolverhampton
SHROPSHIRE
Church Stretton
Bridgnorth
Craven Arms
Ludlow
Kidderminster
Knighton
Droitwich
Presteigne
Leominster
Worcester
Kington
HEREFORD AND WORCESTER
Malvern
Hereford
Ledbury
Tewkesbury
Ross-on-Wye
Cheltenham
Gloucester
Symonds Yat
Cinderford
Abergavenny
Monmouth
GLOUCESTERSHIRE
Stroud
Wotton-under-Edge
Chepstow
Malmesbury
Tormarton
GWENT
Newport
Bristol
Chippenham
Clevedon
AVON
Barmouth
Dolgellau
Welshpool
POWYS
Tywyn
Machynlleth
Montgomery
Newtown
Aberdovey
Llanidloes
Aberystwyth
Rhayader
Llandrindod Wells
Builth Wells
Aberaeron
Painscastle
New Quay
Tregaron
Llanwrtyd Wells
Hay-on-Wye
Lampeter
Brecon
Cardigan
Llandyssul
Llandovery
Newcastle Emlyn
DYFED
Fishguard
St David's
Carmarthen
Llandeilo
Haverfordwest
Broad Haven
Narberth
Milford Haven
Saundersfoot
Merthyr Tydfil
Pembroke
Tenby
Pontypool
Llanelli
WEST GLAMORGAN
MID GLAMORGAN
Swansea
Neath
Pontypridd
Caerphilly
Porthcawl
Bridgend
SOUTH GLAMORGAN
Cardiff
Barry
0 10 20 30 40 50 Kilometres
0 10 20 30 Miles
Grid interval is 30 miles

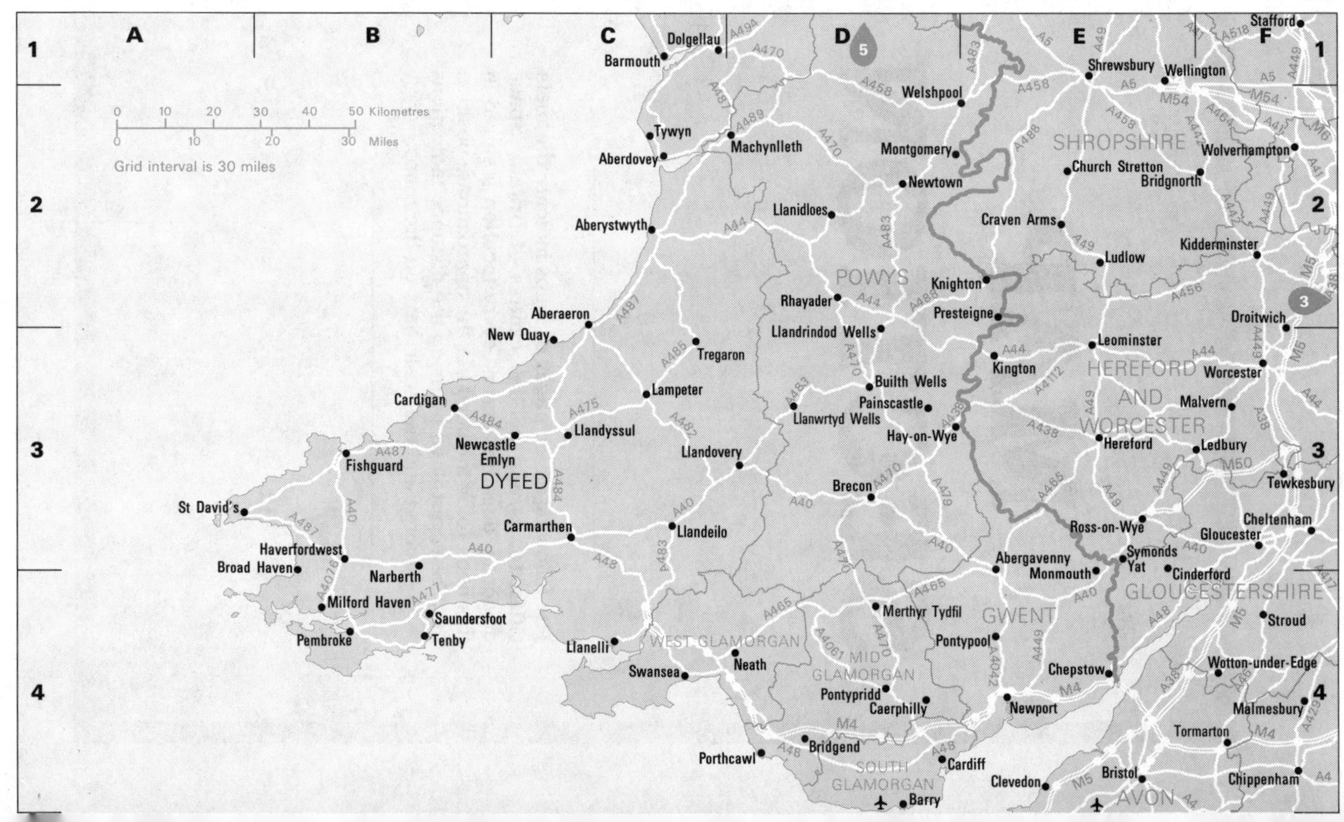

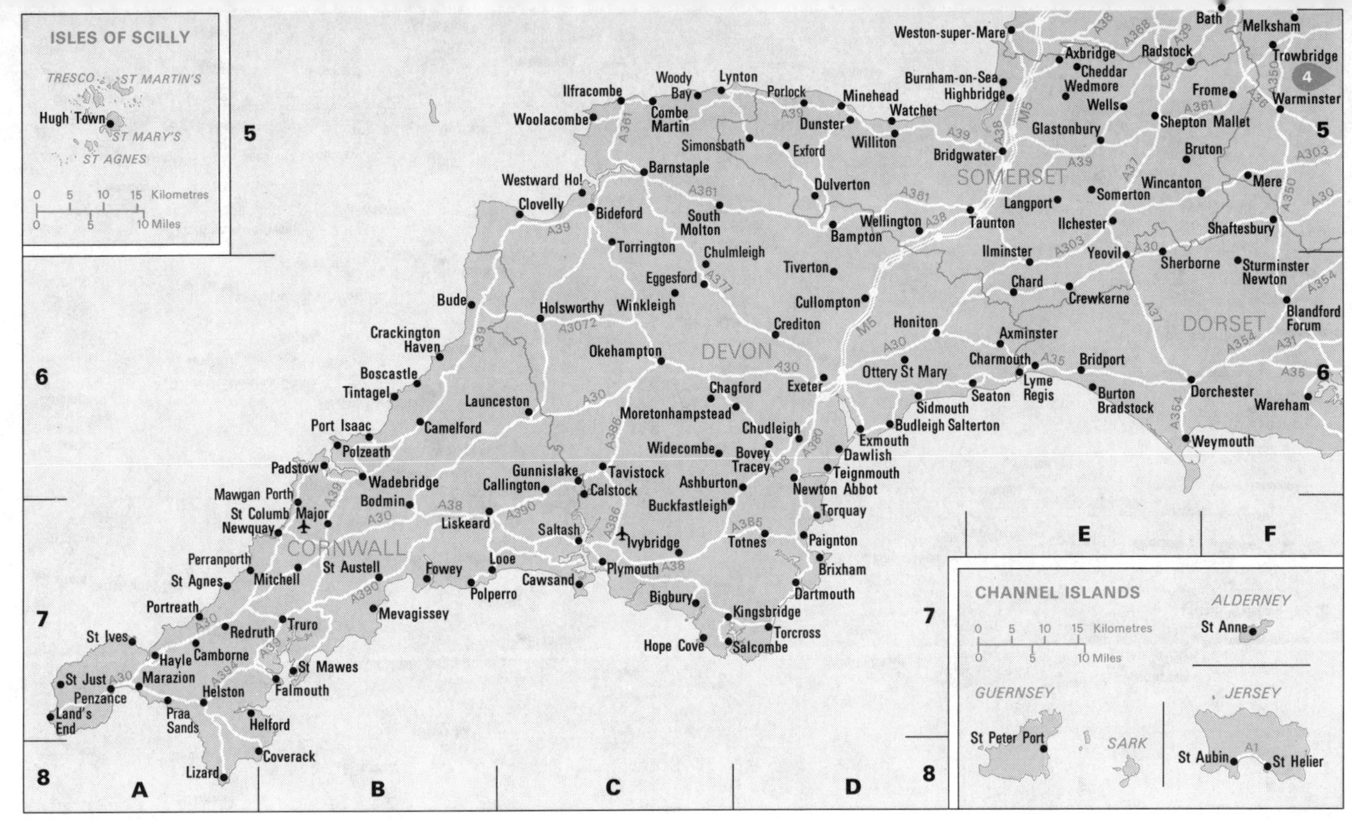
Map 2
ISLES OF SCILLY
TRESCO ST MARTIN'S
ST MARY'S
ST AGNES
Hugh Town
0 5 10 15 Kilometres
0 5 10 Miles
CHANNEL ISLANDS
ALDERNEY
St Anne
0 5 10 15 Kilometres
0 5 10 Miles
GUERNSEY
St Peter Port
SARK
JERSEY
St Aubin
St Helier
SOMERSET
DORSET
DEVON
CORNWALL
Bath
Melksham
Weston-super-Mare
Axbridge
Radstock
Trowbridge
Cheddar
Wedmore
Frome
Warminster
Burnham-on-Sea
Highbridge
Wells
Shepton Mallet
Woody Bay
Lynton
Porlock
Minehead
Watchet
Glastonbury
Bruton
Ilfracombe
Combe Martin
Dunster
Mere
Woolacombe
Simonsbath
Exford
Williton
Bridgwater
Wincanton
Barnstaple
Dulverton
Langport
Somerton
Westward Ho!
Ilchester
Shaftesbury
Clovelly
Bideford
South Molton
Wellington
Taunton
Yeovil
Sherborne
Torrington
Chulmleigh
Bampton
Ilminster
Sturminster Newton
Eggesford
Tiverton
Chard
Crewkerne
Bude
Holsworthy
Winkleigh
Cullompton
Axminster
Blandford Forum
Crackington Haven
Crediton
Honiton
Charmouth
Bridport
Dorchester
Boscastle
Okehampton
DEVON
Ottery St Mary
Lyme Regis
Burton Bradstock
Tintagel
Launceston
Chagford
Exeter
Seaton
Wareham
Port Isaac
Camelford
Moretonhampstead
Sidmouth
Budleigh Salterton
Weymouth
Polzeath
Chudleigh
Exmouth
Padstow
Wadebridge
Gunnislake
Tavistock
Widecombe
Bovey Tracey
Dawlish
Teignmouth
Mawgan Porth
Bodmin
Callington
Calstock
Ashburton
Newton Abbot
St Columb Major
Buckfastleigh
Torquay
Newquay
Liskeard
Saltash
Paignton
CORNWALL
Ivybridge
Totnes
Brixham
Perranporth
St Austell
Fowey
Looe
Plymouth
St Agnes
Mitchell
Cawsand
Dartmouth
Polperro
Bigbury
Portreath
Truro
Mevagissey
Kingsbridge
St Ives
Redruth
Torcross
Hayle
Camborne
Hope Cove
Salcombe
St Just
Marazion
St Mawes
Penzance
Helston
Falmouth
Land's End
Praa Sands
Helford
Lizard
Coverack
5
6
7
8
A
B
C
D
E
F
© GEOprojects (U.K.) Ltd
Crown Copyright Reserved

Map 3

Bakewell
Leek
Matlock
Mansfield
Newark
Skegness
Ashbourne
Nottingham
Sleaford
Boston
Hunstanton
Blakeney
Sheringham
Cromer
Derby
Grantham
Wells-next-the-Sea
Holt
Mundesley-on-Sea
Stafford
Burton-upon-Trent
East Midlands
Spalding
Fakenham
North Walsham
Stalham
Loughborough
Melton Mowbray
King's Lynn
East Dereham
Wroxham
Horning
Hemsby
Lichfield
Leicester
Oakham
Stamford
Downham Market
Swaffham
Norwich
Acle
Great Yarmouth
Uppingham
Peterborough
Watton
Wolverhampton
Lowestoft
Birmingham
Market Harborough
Bungay
Beccles
National Exhibition Centre
Thetford
Diss
Harleston
Coventry
Kettering
Ely
Halesworth
Southwold
Rugby
Huntingdon
Leamington Spa
Bury St Edmunds
Framlingham
Saxmundham
Warwick
Daventry
Northampton
Newmarket
Stratford-upon-Avon
Cambridge
Stowmarket
Aldeburgh
Towcester
Bedford
Haverhill
Lavenham
Woodbridge
Evesham
Sudbury
Hadleigh
Ipswich
Broadway
Banbury
Brackley
Moreton-in-Marsh
Buckingham
Baldock
Dedham
Harwich
Stow-on-the-Wold
Chipping Norton
Hitchin
Colchester
Cheltenham
Kingham
Bicester
Luton
Braintree
Stansted
Dunstable
Bishop's Stortford
Walton-on-Naze
Burford
Aylesbury
Hertford
Clacton-on-Sea

DERBYSHIRE
NOTTINGHAMSHIRE
LINCOLNSHIRE
STAFFS
NORFOLK
LEICESTERSHIRE
WEST MIDLANDS
CAMBRIDGESHIRE
NORTHAMPTONSHIRE
WARWICKSHIRE
SUFFOLK
BEDFORDSHIRE
BUCKS
HERTFORDSHIRE
ESSEX
GLOS

A B C D E F
1 2 3 4 6

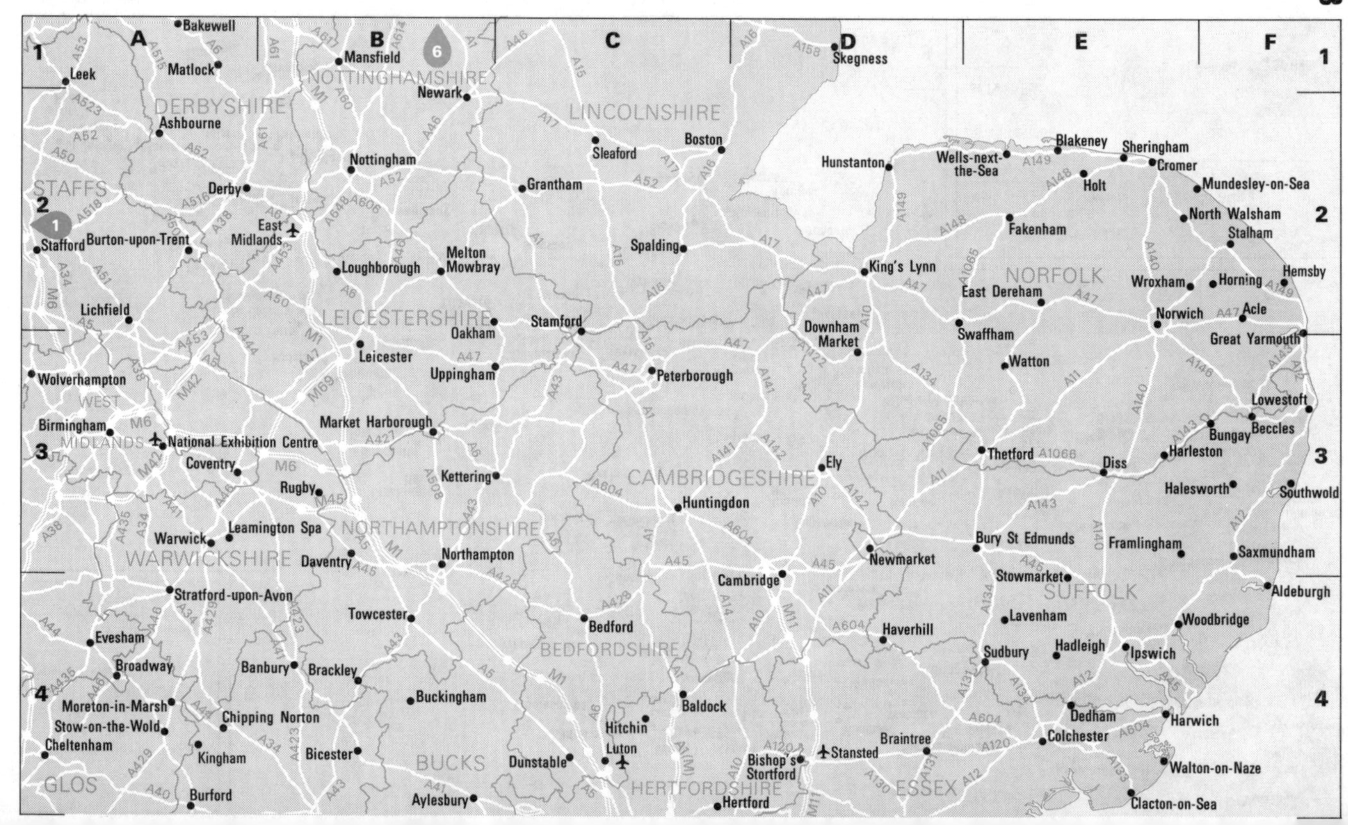

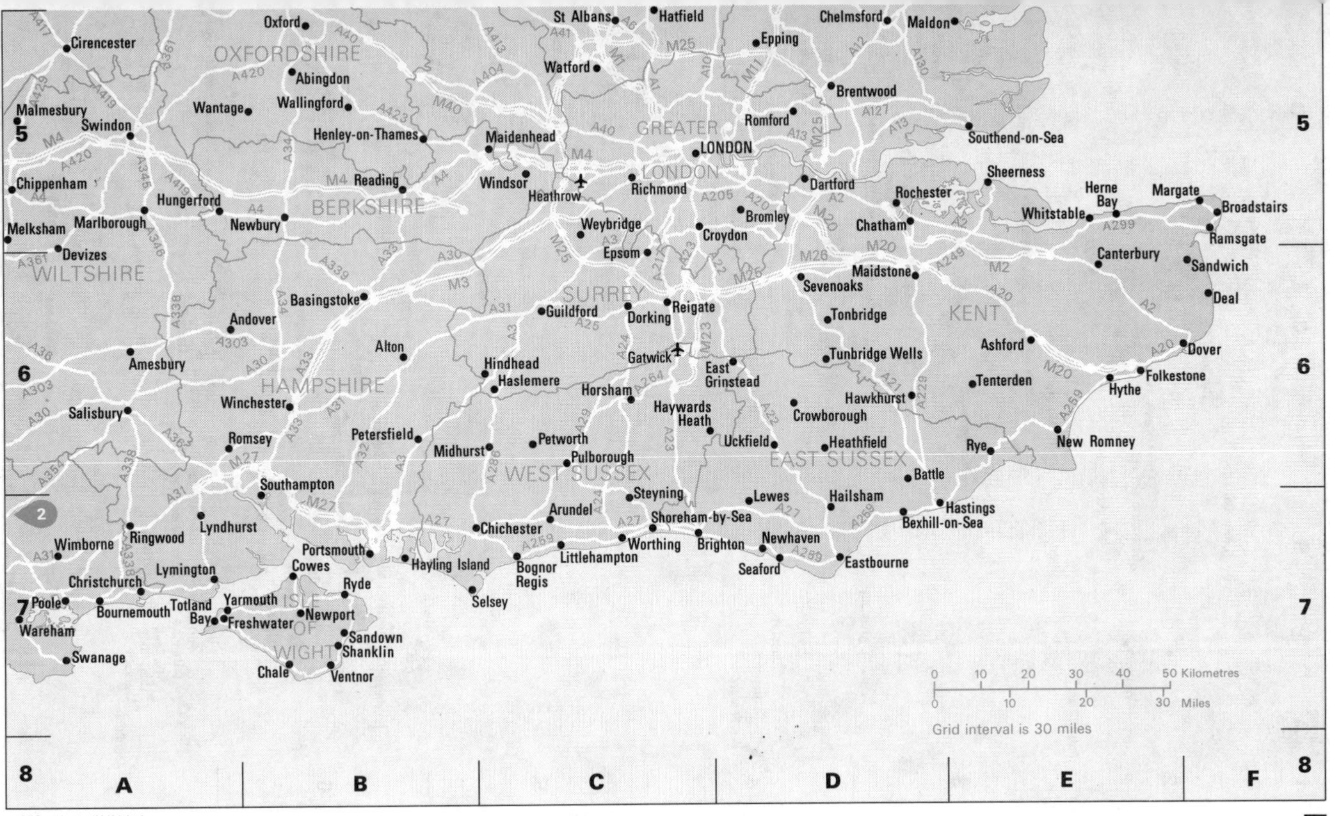

© GEOprojects (U.K.) Ltd
Crown Copyright Reserved

Map 5

© GEOprojects (U.K.) Ltd
Crown Copyright Reserved

Map 6

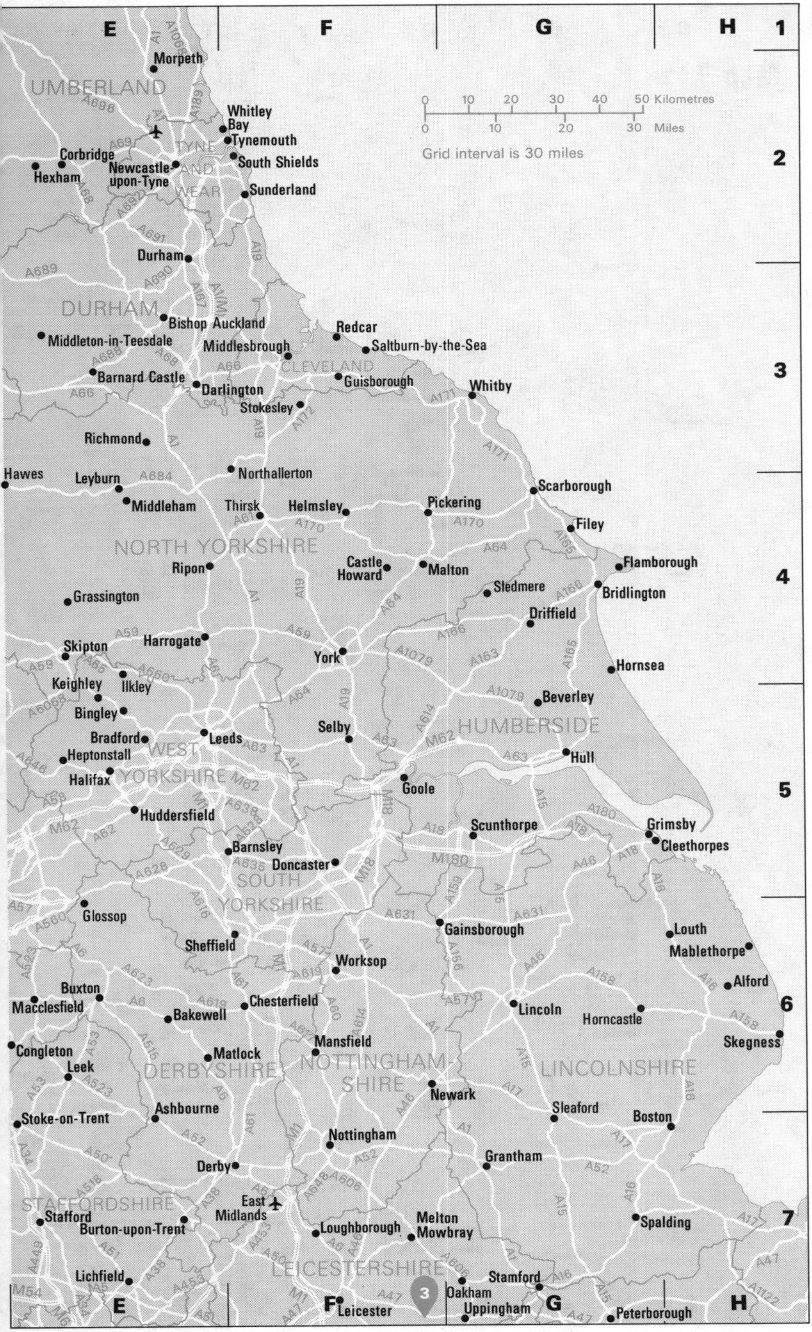

E
F
G
H
1
2
3
4
5
6
7

0 10 20 30 40 50 Kilometres
0 10 20 30 Miles
Grid interval is 30 miles

Morpeth
UMBERLAND
Whitley Bay
Tynemouth
Corbridge
South Shields
Hexham
Newcastle upon-Tyne
TYNE AND WEAR
Sunderland
Durham
DURHAM
Bishop Auckland
Middleton-in-Teesdale
Middlesbrough
Redcar
Saltburn-by-the-Sea
Barnard Castle
CLEVELAND
Guisborough
Whitby
Darlington
Stokesley
Richmond
Northallerton
Scarborough
Hawes
Leyburn
Middleham
Thirsk
Helmsley
Pickering
Filey
NORTH YORKSHIRE
Flamborough
Ripon
Castle Howard
Malton
Bridlington
Grassington
Sledmere
Driffield
Skipton
Harrogate
Hornsea
Keighley
Ilkley
York
Beverley
Bingley
Selby
HUMBERSIDE
Bradford
Leeds
Heptonstall
Hull
Halifax
WEST YORKSHIRE
Goole
Huddersfield
Grimsby
Barnsley
Scunthorpe
Cleethorpes
Doncaster
SOUTH YORKSHIRE
Glossop
Gainsborough
Louth
Sheffield
Mablethorpe
Worksop
Alford
Buxton
Chesterfield
Lincoln
Macclesfield
Bakewell
Horncastle
Skegness
Congleton
Matlock
Leek
DERBYSHIRE
NOTTINGHAM-SHIRE
LINCOLNSHIRE
Mansfield
Ashbourne
Newark
Sleaford
Stoke-on-Trent
Boston
Nottingham
Grantham
Derby
East Midlands
Spalding
STAFFORDSHIRE
Stafford
Melton Mowbray
Burton-upon-Trent
Loughborough
Lichfield
LEICESTERSHIRE
Stamford
Oakham
Leicester
Uppingham
Peterborough

© GEOprojects (U.K.) Ltd
Crown Copyright Reserved